HE
Husb... 02. FEB 95

C000185856

990920603 X

T H E
VILLAGE
SHOW

THE
VILLAGE
SHOW

URSULA BUCHAN

PHOTOGRAPHS BY HUGH PALMER

PAVILION

ACKNOWLEDGEMENTS

I am immensely grateful to the flower show. Without it, I might never have become a gardening writer. In the autumn of 1984, I submitted an article to *The Spectator*, based on my experiences as a vegetable judge at our village show. It became the first of many monthly articles I have written since for that periodical. In the spring of 1987, a chance comment about that first article in The *Observer* caught the attention of two television film directors, Peter Carr and Maxine Baker, and led to my presenting two six-part series of 'Village Show', which were made by Granada Television for Channel Four.

In the process of helping to make those programmes, my fascination with flower shows, and my respect for the gardeners who exhibit at them, grew enormously. I therefore owe a great debt of gratitude to Granada for giving me the opportunity to meet so many good exhibitors and for providing the basic research from which this book grew.

I should also like to thank Jack Wood, who has been, for nearly thirty years, shows reporter for *Garden News*. His knowledge of flower shows, large and small, is second to none and he shared that knowledge unstintingly. I am very grateful to Dr Brent Elliott (Librarian), Susanne Mitchell and Allan Sawyer, all of the Royal Horticultural Society, Mary Newnes and Major Geoffrey Bevan for answering my many questions so patiently. I should also like to thank Denise Simmons for lightening the domestic load.

My task was made the easier by the ready assistance of the various show societies and, in particular, the show secretaries: Meriel Jones of the Abergavenny and Border Counties Agricultural Society, Tommy Moffat of the Dumfries and Lockerbie Agricultural Society, Sheila Davies of the Aberystwyth and District Agricultural Society, Jim and Joan Turner of the Warmington Horticultural Society, Keith and Janet Pulman of the North Somerset Agricultural Society, and Lieutenant-Colonel Ken Grapes of the Royal National Rose Society.

My thanks go to the Royal Horticultural Society for permission to quote from the 1981 edition of *The Horticultural Show Handbook*; to Faber and Faber for the extract from Philip Larkin's 'Show Saturday' and David and Charles for the quotation from *Growing and Showing Roses*.

I am enormously grateful to Hugh Palmer for capturing so well in pictures what I have struggled to express in prose. Once again I thank my husband, Charles Wide, for his non-interference, offers to mind children, and purchase of *his own* word processor, and to Emily and Thomas for their precocious forbearance.

Most of all, I should like to thank all the exhibitors and judges who appear in these pages, for their unflagging helpfulness, their willingness to unfold the secrets of their craft and their touching, if probably misplaced, faith in my ability to tell their stories. To them, and to their spouses who provided such sustaining home-made refreshments at all hours of the day, this book is respectfully, and affectionately, dedicated.

First published in Great Britain in 1990 by
Pavilion Books Limited
196 Shaftesbury Avenue, London WC2H 8JL

Text copyright © 1990 Ursula Buchan · Photographs copyright © 1990 Hugh Palmer
Designed by Janet James

All rights reserved. No part of this publication may be reproduced,
stored in a retrieval system or transmitted in any form or by any means,
electronic, mechanical, photocopying, recording or otherwise, without
the prior permission of the copyright holder.

ISBN 1 85145 435 7
10 9 8 7 6 5 4 3 2 1
Printed and bound in Spain by Graficas Estella

GLOUCESTERSHIRE
CLASS COPY
COUNTY LIBRARY

CONTENTS

PREFACE 6
INTRODUCTION 9

This book is the result of conversations conducted with some of the horticultural exhibitors, and one or two judges and show organisers, whom I first met while helping to make the television series, 'Village Show'. These took place in the spring and summer of 1989 as the exhibitors were preparing for shows in Abergavenny, Dumfries, Aberystwyth, Warmington in Northamptonshire, north Somerset and Cumbria. It was possible, during the course of those leisurely conversations, to delve rather more deeply into the subject of showing and shows than could be the case, rather naturally, in six short television programmes.

The choice of show was governed by my desire to include a wide range of subject matter, exhibitors and geographical regions, within the necessarily limited compass of an average-sized book. However necessary, it was nevertheless very painful to have to leave out the stories of many interesting showmen that I have met, and good shows that I have attended. All but one of the shows described is essentially local in atmosphere. Fascinating as national competitions can be, their very seriousness can militate against enjoyment, and it is the fun of showing which I particularly wished to illustrate. The only exception in the book, put in for comparison, is the Lakeland Rose Show. Whether because the financial rewards at this show are so comparatively modest for a national competition or because roses attract a particularly outgoing breed of competitor, this is a show which seems to combine the best features of the local show with the unbeatable expertise expected at a national event.

Not all the shows described are village events, of course, because in the average village show there are likely to be only two or three good competitors, and I wished the salt of competition to season the dry bread of description. However, even the two county shows are local in feeling. It is the willingness on the part of showmen to travel long distances, stay overnight, and give up their entire summer in the pursuit of excellence, which makes national shows so different. Anyone will tell you as a matter of pride that there is as good stuff exhibited at their local show as is to be found in the national shows (just as they will tell you that there are as pretty girls in their street as any entering the 'Miss World' competition) and that boast is, I am convinced, justified as far as, say, the vegetables at Abergavenny or the begonias in Dumfriesshire are concerned. The difference is that it does not occur to most of the local exhibitors in Abergavenny or Dumfries to consider exhibiting nationally. Anyone who does is driven not by a greater desire for perfection but a rare energy and drive to succeed – like Don Charlton and Tom Foster with their roses.

I concentrated on three main aspects of the exhibitors' experience: their life history in as much as it shed light on why they showed; their methods of cultivation and in particular of preparation for shows; and the day itself. I have assumed a basic knowledge of gardening on the part of the reader; it would have been impossible otherwise to have kept the book within bounds, and its usefulness for potential exhibitors would have been seriously undermined. It is intended that anyone fired with enthusiasm to show cacti and succulents, floral art, roses, vegetables, begonias, fuchsias, fruit, or their garden should find plenty of helpful information in these pages.

I am glad to say that this book is not, strictly speaking, a practical manual, but rather contains the personal experiences of a variety of showmen, always individual and occasionally downright idiosyncratic in their opinions. The information should not therefore be taken as being applicable to all gardeners in all regions on all soils. Nevertheless, the fact that these showmen are successful ones, in the running for first prizes and even cups each year, means that their comments can be taken seriously. However, those readers who would like a purely practical instruction book need look no further than the excellent *Growing for Showing* series published by David and Charles, which contains volumes on vegetables, fuchsias, chrysanthemums, dahlias, geraniums and roses. For those who want a general book, and who exhibit at August shows, *Growing for Showing* by George Whitehead (Faber and Faber) is ideal. Many books concerned with a particular genus, such as *Growing Begonias* by Eric Catterall (Croom Helm), have helpful and informative chapters on exhibiting. Lastly, would-be competitive flower arrangers will find their questions answered by Howard Franklin's *A Flower Arranger's Guide to Showing* (Batsford).

It cannot be ignored that, although the frankness shown to me was remarkable and affecting, taking note of all that these showmen say may not make the reader a show winner. Apart from the fact that some people definitely are better than others at gardening I should certainly not have blamed anyone whom I met if they had held back some important detail, not wishing it to be widely broadcast. I certainly encountered very little hesitancy in the answering of my many questions, but that is rather different from the volunteering of information not specifically requested.

Nor must it be forgotten that memories, even of past glories, can fade. I always used a tape recorder to record conversations and I have tried as hard as is in my power to check all facts, but it is not beyond the realms of possibility that there were one or two misunderstandings which have led to error. If there are, I apologise.   U.B.

Minute examination of leek 'beards' by the judges at Abergavenny Show.

INTRODUCTION

On August Bank Holiday Monday, 1987, I put nine small shallots in the 'shallots, pickling, 9' class at my local flower show. I knew exactly what to do – and so I should, for not only had I been taught what to look for by an experienced judge, but I had just spent the best part of the summer talking to horticultural exhibitors. I picked out as many round bulbs as I could, measured them with a home-made inch-diameter metal ring to check their rotundity and size, and stripped each onion of its broken outer skin, being careful not to skin them as far as the shiny white layers beneath. I picked out the most uniform nine, turned down their short necks, tied these neatly and tightly with thin elastic, placed them on dry builder's sand on a paper plate, and carried them, with bitten lip and deliberate tread, to the show tent. Several times before the judging began, I checked neurotically to see that there really were nine of them, just in case one should have mysteriously disappeared into the ether.

My knowledge of the way things work, rather than the superior quality of my shallots, won me a handsome red first prize card and a fifty pence piece. Nothing all season gave me quite so much pleasure. I was bitten, as they say, by the bug. I had become a showman.

Even before I held my breath and jumped in, however, I had acted as a steward or trainee judge at local shows, and had enjoyed the businesslike calm which surrounded the judges as they did their work and, after the show opened, the smell of trampled grass mingling with Victoria sponge and roses, accompanied by the sound of onlookers giving their unflattering opinions in stage-whispers.

I understand, therefore, the impulse which drives people not only to give up so much of their leisure time in the pursuit of horticultural excellence but to demonstrate that excellence to their neighbours. This single-minded concentration may sometimes be obsessive but it is not mad, as some people maintain in a tone of patronizing amusement. I have met dozens of showmen (I use the word to mean women as well as men, it goes without saying) all over mainland Britain, but I can honestly say that I never saw a staring eye, a frothing mouth or a trembling hand. Indeed what impressed me most about them was their ability to laugh at themselves.

Showing, and winning, fulfill a perfectly natural desire to be the best at something: those who can afford it own racehorses, those who are young and fit play football, those who are neither young nor rich show the produce which, with consummate skill, they have tended in their gardens. That does not seem to me to be a cause for derisory laughter. Quite the reverse. There are few activities which are a better blend of worthy mental and physical exertion than growing plants to perfection. And, having grown them, why should they not show them off?

Showmen are by no means a homogeneous group but they seem to have certain characteristics in common. They often have dull jobs, or no job at all, and are rarely very successful in the world's eyes; showing, therefore, satisfies a need (which we all have) to succeed, or, at the very least, to be respected by those whom we respect.

They have often spent time in the services, either during the last war or, afterwards, at the time of compulsory National Service. That may say more about their age than anything else, but it is no coincidence that certain attributes learned in the services – self-discipline, orderliness, a high boredom threshold – are helpful traits for aspiring exhibitors. There are certainly successful exhibitors who are quite young (two youthful professional gardeners appear in these pages) but the time needed to do the job perfectly means that only those young people who are very keen can succeed, even at a local level.

Perhaps because of their average age, showmen are a conservative lot, occasionally given to adventurous leaps into the unknown but, on the whole, happier sticking to the old ways and following a set routine each year. That is not to say that they are unreceptive to new ideas, only that these must accord with their experience. They have often left school at the earliest opportunity, so much of what they know they have taught themselves or learned later at evening classes; they therefore exhibit the self-reliance of those who know they have learned the hard way and a certain disdain for those who have not.

Most seem free of self-doubt, which is as well for it would substantially undermine their effectiveness if they ever asked themselves the point of what they were doing. This is particularly true, naturally enough, of exhibitors who compete at a national level.

Most striking of all is their almost infinite capacity for taking pains, even when their aspirations go no further than small local shows. They are immensely hard-working, prepared, in the pursuit of perfection, to contemplate work which seriously curtails television watching, cuts down on social life, and determines the timing of holidays, or even whether holidays are taken at all. It is no coincidence that many have a good-natured wife (or husband) who will not only tolerate the restrictions put on social life and travel by this all-absorbing occupation, but be prepared to pinch out the side shoots of sweet peas on summer evenings or hold pots upright in the car on the way to the show.

One must resist the temptation to be dewy-eyed about all exhibitors. There are some very bad sports, and not just in the large competitions where the size of the prizes or the magnitude of the prestige could be expected to cause the participants to lose their sense of humour. There are single-minded, selfish 'pot hunters' too. At the smallest of village shows, fusses are not uncommon, rivals' produce can be spoiled, and cheating occurs. That said, it is remarkable how many showmen do all that work simply for the glory, lose cheerfully, and do not even bother to collect their prize money, which, at least on the level of village and small agricultural shows, is usually very small anyway.

Little has been written about the history of the small flower show, but it does seem that the ground was laid by the florists' societies which flourished in the eighteenth and early nineteenth centuries. The word 'florist' refers to someone who grew one of eight specified flowers: auricula, polyanthus, ranunculus, carnation, anemone, tulip, hyacinth, or pink. These were grown by the strictest of rules and to the peak of perfection, often by artisans in towns. The florists' societies were usually based in public houses, and held 'feasts' when their particular pet was in flower and could be shown and criticized. Such perfectionism has never been surpassed. By the 1830s, the pansy and the dahlia had joined the ranks of recognized florists' flowers, and were followed by the chrysanthemum and other flowers. By 1860, however, many old-established florists' societies based in pubs were suffering a slow decline, probably from a general impatience with their restrictions.

From the 1830s, there was a marked growth in the numbers of villa and suburban gardens, as the better-off began to leave the centres of cities. General gardening was becoming very popular and professional gardeners were employed in large numbers by the well-to-do. A host of new magazines and periodicals appeared to service this burgeoning interest. Hundreds of general horticultural societies were founded, in cities, towns and the country. The Horticultural Society of London was established in 1804, held its first show in 1830, and received royal recognition in 1860, when it was renamed the Royal Horticultural Society. It set a standard for local groups to follow. At the present time there are well over 2,500 horticultural societies in Britain affiliated to the Royal Horticultural Society and many more that are not.

These horticultural societies were heavily supported by professional gardeners, often very competitive, so these societies soon began holding their own shows. Often the impetus or encouragement in villages came from a benevolently paternalistic gentry who would provide prizes and perhaps a field for the marquee. The clergy also took an active part. It was thought very beneficial for the cottagers to participate in order to improve their gardens (and their moral well-being). This was the time when the allotment movement was in full swing, so many people (both in villages and towns) had substantial plots of land to cultivate. There were usually classes in the shows specifically for 'cottagers' or 'parishioners', and also classes for professional gardeners working on estates, who vied with those from other large houses to produce the most perfect and exotic exhibits. Although the traditional florists' flowers were still grown and shown, it was the enormous increase in popularity of the dahlia, the chrysanthemum, and vegetables which tended to settle the date of the local show on a day in August or early September. Sometimes there would be sufficient interest for a midsummer rose and sweet pea show as well.

There are still in existence horticultural societies which were founded well over a hundred years ago and which have held flower shows ever since. For example, the Nailsea Show was founded in the 1850s to raise

money for the war wounded of the Crimea. Many agricultural societies also date from the Victorian era: the North Somerset Agricultural Society for example, has existed for more than 150 years and held shows annually for most of that time.

The general flower show, as we know, contains much non-horticultural produce such as handicrafts, artwork, photographs, honey, home-made wine and children's cookery (not to mention the seemingly obligatory pink crocheted loo-roll covers), thus making the name 'flower show' something of a misnomer. However, the 'florists'' type of show has also survived in some places. The best known of this kind are the 'pot' leek or onion shows in County Durham and Northumberland run by clubs which are based, like the old florists' societies, in pubs; the gooseberry competitions around Goosetrey and Holmes Chapel in Cheshire; auricula shows around Middleton in Manchester (where they have always been strong) and old garden varieties of tulips at Wakefield. Because there is no centralized direction of shows, and they have grown up willy-nilly, there is much local variation.

On a national scale there are societies which are concerned with flower arranging, primulas and auriculas,

Amy Harbour's flower garden at Warmington in Northamptonshire, an entry in 'the best garden' competition.

pelargoniums and geraniums, carnations and pinks, delphiniums, roses, sweet peas, dahlias, chrysanthemums, alpines, and even 'pot' leeks. They all have national shows, often staged in London. Just down the scale there are many regional groups, such as the Lancashire and Cheshire Carnation Society.

The heyday of the local general flower show is thought to have been the early years of this century, when there were so few other forms of entertainment open to the working classes, particularly in the country. It is highly unlikely that the quality of produce was any higher than today, for modern showmen can reap the benefits of a hundred years of selective plant breeding, but the influence of local head gardeners undoubtedly meant that the range of exhibits, particularly of glasshouse fruit, was more extensive. This can clearly be seen in the photographs reproduced in Charles H. Curtis's *The Book of the Flower Show* (1910). (Apart from the range of produce, what is remarkable about this book, which is a practical manual of instruction for would-be showmen, is how *little* has changed, especially in the way produce is presented, since 1910). By the First World War, the nascent cinema had become an important rival interest. Even today, however, flower shows are being founded, or at least resurrected.

Although I hesitate about generalizing, particularly when evidence is often anecdotal and therefore hard to substantiate, it would seem that these days flower shows are relatively strongest, per head of population, in the north and west. As showing can be a solace in bad times, shows tend to flourish in regions where traditional industries, such as mining and steel working, are threatened and unemployment is high, like the north-east of England and South Wales. The flower show is most under pressure as a result of falling entries, in the prosperous south and east (though there are many honourable exceptions, of course). Now that we are a nation of car-owners, the local flower show must compete for our attention with dozens of other activities. For many, reared on television, the flower show now seems rather unsophisticated, although it celebrates skills more marvellous than those exhibited in game shows.

All shows have had to adjust to changing circumstances, often bringing in sideshows to attract the casual onlooker, and committees have felt compelled to change the rather traditional nature of show schedules to encourage a new type of exhibitor. The introduction of flower arrangement classes, usually well-supported, is an example of a response to popular demand.

Flower shows, like showmen, exhibit a sturdy individualism, yet have much in common. Schedules all differ from each other: in prize money offered, in rules about 'open' and 'restricted' classes, how to apply for entries, how many entries are allowed, what time to stage, what time to judge, how points are assessed, the width of frontage of vegetable collections, when to collect produce – in fact, in a hundred minute particulars. Nevertheless, in essentials they are the same, because the vast majority of show committees follow the rules laid down, or the advice proffered, in *The Horticultural Show Handbook: For the guidance of organizers, schedule-makers, exhibitors, and judges* (revised 1981), published by the Royal Horticultural Society. This is 'the exhibitor's Bible' and no serious competitor can afford to be without it.

It is presently in the process of being revised once more. Let us hope that the charm of the old Handbook will remain undiminished in the new edition. I should be particularly sorry ever to see the end of the two paragraphs *'Prizes not Everything'* and *'Be a Sportsman'*. The latter states: *'The judges' decision, whatever it may be, should be accepted with good grace. An exhibitor who has failed to get a prize and cannot at once see why, should search calmly and patiently for the cause of his competitors' success so that he, himself, may be successful another time.'*

It is fun to compare that with Curtis's remarks on 'Protests' in 1910: *'"Judging the judges" is a favourite pursuit of amateur and professional gardeners alike, at Horticultural Shows. The gardener is only human and when the subjects of his consideration are those that he himself has cultivated, it is pardonable if we find him unwilling at times*

to accept an unfavourable verdict. The angry competitor, like irate persons in many other circumstances, does not always count the proverbial sixty ere making a protest, or if he does stay to count sixty, he finds his chagrin to increase.' Plus ça change . . .

Many shows are judged specifically 'under RHS rules' but even if they are not, judges, organizers of shows, and exhibitors use the Handbook as guide and mentor. That being the case, I shall summarize its most important rules in order not to have to do so in much detail in the following chapters.

'Unless otherwise stated in the schedule', exhibits must be the property of the exhibitor, and must have been in his possession for at least two months. There should only be one exhibitor from one garden (a rule disregarded by many showmen who often put extra exhibits in the show in their spouse's name), and exhibits must contain only the quantity specified (too few or too many is 'Not According to Schedule'). There is a long list in the Handbook of how many of each type of exhibit constitutes a 'dish' but show committees often suit themselves about this; in small shows, for example, asking for thirty raspberries or thirty-six Brussels sprouts is asking for an empty bench.

All exhibits should be correctly named: *'Errors in naming will not disqualify the entry but the judges should regard correctness and clearness of naming as telling in favour*

of an exhibit in a close competition.' Prizes may be withheld or modified, if the exhibits are considered unworthy of the prize offered, and, of course, the judges' decision is final. A disputes procedure, involving the complainant in depositing a cash sum, returned if the complaint is found to be justified, is laid down.

There are other rules but these are the main ones applicable to all shows and they have evolved and been refined over the years after due consultation with a variety of judges, organizers, and, of course, exhibitors. There is much advice about the presentation and staging of produce at flower shows, which will find a place in the ensuing chapters. There is also a very useful section on definitions, everything from 'bowl' to 'cultivar', 'salad-ing' to 'professional'.

As a general rule, judges look for variations on four features, whatever the exhibit: condition, size, colour, and uniformity. Each, or some of these, attract points which together add up to a certain total, for instance twenty for potatoes, or twenty-five for daffodils. As well as the four basic features, there are other facets, which may change from subject to subject. For example, there

LEFT One of the prizewinners in the Grand Parade at Aberystwyth Show.

RIGHT The ancient skills of cutting and laying a hedge being displayed in the hedging competition at the North Somerset Ploughing Match.

are four points allocated for the consideration of 'eyes' in potatoes, whereas, in daffodils, three points are allocated for poise, three for texture and two for the stems.

Some plants are easier to grow than others and so attract fewer maximum points; in the case of grapes (as will be seen in chapter 5) there are even different maximum points available, depending on the cultivar. The system of 'pointage' matters most when a 'collection' of fruit or vegetables is being judged, but I find, as a novice judge, that in well-supported classes of *individual* items, using the points system can help decide the order of places.

Together with accounts of the amount of points available, the Handbook also lists features of each type of exhibit which are either meritorious or defective. This information is invaluable, even to the experienced judge.

To be a good judge takes enormous experience, keen powers of decision, a methodical approach, fairminded-ness and simple humanity. Because of the steep decline since the last war in the number of professional garden-ers, most committees do have difficulty from time to time finding such paragons.

The training of local judges is various. It ranges from none at all, through learning from another judge, to taking (and passing) the exacting exams set each year by one of the specialist societies, such as the National Vegetable Society or the National Dahlia Society. In my

experience, judges at local shows take their duties remarkably seriously and do a thoughtful, thorough task; complaints against them are often not justified except as an exhibition of sour grapes. What is more, they usually do the job for no payment and sometimes not even for expenses or lunch. It is still considered by judges an honour to be asked (a recognition of one's expertise which may, however, be rather illusory in districts where an expert horticultural judge is as rare a bird as the black-tailed godwit).

Each judge is accompanied by at least one steward, usually a knowledgeable member of the show committee, whose job it is to check that the exhibitors have made no mistakes before the time for staging is over (not done as much as it could be), banishing competitors at judging time, and seeing that all entry cards are placed face down so that the judge cannot know the identity of exhibitors. They usually also carry the results of the judging to the rest of the committee, sitting round a table, who have the laborious task of noting all the winners, counting up the points, and writing out the prize cards – usually red for first, blue for second, yellow for third.

As well as deciding on the relative merits of the exhibits, judges have also to look out for any sign of cheating. Cheating undoubtedly happens at all levels of showing, although I suspect there is a great deal less of it than is popularly imagined. Most exhibitors do not

bother, either because they are honest or because they know that these things are very hard to disguise. In the course of my conversations with both exhibitors and judges, I was told stories of how (other) people put soap in slug holes in potatoes, inserted florist's wire carefully to stiffen a daffodil head, put fresh florets in the middle of chrysanthemum flowers, pinned fresh gladiolus flowers onto a 'blowing' spike, drew crayon markings on 'Catriona' potatoes, stuck skin onto onions with glue, even bought vegetables from shops or 'pick-your-own' farms. I imagine that judges are occasionally taken in by these devices, but far less often than the unscrupulous exhibitor fondly supposes. The judge's reaction is to write 'NAS' (Not According to Schedule) and his reasons on the card next to the dubious exhibit. Once a man has a reputation as a cheat amongst his fellows, his time at shows becomes markedly less convivial.

There is a distinction to be drawn, however, between enhancing an exhibit and trying to deceive the judge. Exhibitors use milk to wash their potatoes in order to give them a richer cream colour; this is known and accepted. What is not acceptable is using soap to disguise a slug hole. The subject does involve judge and exhibitor in a line-drawing exercise, it has to be said.

As well as cheating at shows, there are instances of rivals' produce being damaged before it ever gets there, and it is not uncommon for big-time growers to sleep on their allotments to prevent this. Curiously, it seems that some types of produce attract more dishonest and unscrupulous competitors than others, and there is no doubt that the size of prize money has a bearing on this.

Much of the useful information that showmen absorb comes not from books, which are thought to be expensive and quick to date, but from the gardening press, most particularly *Garden News*. Like a tabloid newspaper in format, it is cheap and very up-to-date.

The information is especially sophisticated in the area of chemicals (showmen are not yet convinced of the efficacy of organic gardening, although if they were to discover that it gave them the same or better results for less money they would embrace it wholeheartedly). They usually have a prodigious armoury of pesticides and, while the nation's gardeners buy a bag of 'Growmore' each year to sprinkle on everything, showmen are ordering 'Chempak No. 8' and mixing their own potting composts.

Exhibitors also use *Garden News* to advertise their strains of 'pot' leeks ('"ex 70 cubic inch stock" £10 per dozen') or twenty-two inch runner beans, of which much of course is promised. *Garden News* sponsors a vegetable 'collection' class at participating local flower shows called the *Garden News* 'Top Tray'. Entrants have the chance of winning gold, silver, or bronze medal and a cash prize. It usually attracts the best efforts of vegetable growers, and it is with vegetables that we begin.

CHAPTER ONE

ABERGAVENNY

Abergavenny and Border Counties Agricultural
Society's Annual Show

The ancient town of Abergavenny, with its ruined Norman castle built on the site of a Roman fort, stands above the River Usk where this famous salmon-river widens out after passing through the Brecon Beacons. The town is set in a ring of hills, most striking of which are the Sugar Loaf to the north, Skirrid Fawr (the Holy Mountain) to the east, and Blorenge to the south. The Romans chose it as a settlement partly because it has a more favoured climate than anywhere further up the valleys. Abergavenny is not only 'the gateway to Wales' but an important centre for the rural hinterland; there are regular sheep and cattle markets, and horse and pony sales.

Abergavenny Show certainly reflects local pre-occupations. It is organized by the Abergavenny and Border Counties Agricultural Society and is held on the last Saturday in July in fields at Llanwenarth, a hamlet just outside the town. The atmosphere is similar to that of Aberystwyth (see chapter 3): it is a rural show offering a mixture of horse and farm livestock classes, an 'open' dog show, a tent for handicrafts and one for horticultural produce. Among the highlights of the day's entertainment in 1989 were the trotting races, a 'stuntarama', the Inter-Counties Mounted Games, and the parade of the Monmouthshire hounds. There is a Grand Parade of cattle, sheep, goats, horses and dogs in the afternoon. The strong classes in the Horticultural Marquee are the sweet peas, roses, floral art, and vegetables.

If there is one kind of produce which seems to epitomize the local flower show, at least for those who take only a passing interest in the subject, it is vegetables. Whenever flower shows are being made fun of (and they often are), it is the huge onions, giant leeks, gigantic marrows and gargantuan pumpkins which are the butt of every joke. Nothing has so damaged the reputation of exhibitors, or more effectively deterred potential exhibitors, than the showman's seeming predilection for outsize, and apparently inedible vegetables.

It is also part of our folklore to expect all vegetable showmen to be 'old boys', prepared to employ every kind of desperate, and usually illegal, device to win with these mammoth, useless vegetables. (I remember that the first, and only one-act play I ever wrote, at the age of eleven, concerned a village show where a giant marrow, cultivated by the white-whiskered vicar, deflated when the first prize rosette was pinned to it. This caused the vicar much consternation, but it was only to be expected from a green and white painted balloon. At this distance in time, it occurs to me that I must have got the idea from somewhere.)

However, I discovered when I visited vegetable gardeners preparing for Abergavenny Show that fact and fiction hardly anywhere converge. Indeed, even the view that vegetable exhibiting is confined to 'old boys' is an over-simplification. They are male, certainly, but, in my experience at least, not more than middle-aged.

It is not surprising that they are usually men, for vegetable growing is traditionally the man's province and old habits of that kind die hard in the country. 'The wife does the flower garden and I do a bit with the vegetables', is a sentence that I have heard a hundred times. Vegetable gardening can be hard physical labour, even on light soils, particularly as the best growers will not use rotavators. Although vegetable gardens *can* be aesthetically pleasing, that is a secondary consideration; it is far more often an unrelievedly practical occupation giving endless opportunities for the ingenious and thrifty construction of polythene and wooden structures. Many women find vegetable gardening a satisfying retreat from the vexed creative questions which daily tug at them in the flower garden, but they would far rather eat (or as often freeze) than show the fruits of their labours. It would seem that it is predominantly men that find beauty in a beetroot and poetry in a parsnip. That is not to say that men do not like flowers as well, but the ones they seem to favour are what one might call 'big production number' flowers which need unremitting attention, such as dahlias, sweet peas and chrysanthemums: colourful versions of twenty-point vegetables in fact.

The most successful vegetable growers in the Abergavenny district are not old, but all, for one reason or another such as early retirement, have a certain amount of time available to them for pursuing intensive vegetable growing. Wilf Mayo, for example, is a jobbing gardener and school bus driver. He lives with his wife, Doreen, in Llanvetherine, a small village in the beautiful hilly country on the edge of the Black Mountains and close to Offa's Dyke, a few miles east of Abergavenny. He is softly-spoken and naturally modest, with an understated sense of humour; his wife is talkative and outgoing. They have the old country courtesy and sense of hospitality.

Born in 1933, the son of a farmworker, he has never,

apart from a short spell on a farm in Herefordshire and his time doing National Service, strayed far from the valley. He worked at various local farms until, in 1964, he and his wife were given the chance of a council house in Llanvetherine, and here they have remained ever since. His father lives next door.

Wilf has always enjoyed gardening and showing. Many years ago he was a member of the village Produce Association in Llanvetherine. He found, however, that as time went by, he began to win all the prizes at the show and it was becoming a decidedly one-sided affair. A little embarrassed by his conspicuous success, he started to go further afield – Abergavenny, Cross Ash, Monmouth, Llangattock Lingoed, Pandy – to meet the competition that he felt he needed.

In 1961 he went to work on a farm at Llanvapley, about three miles from Llanvetherine. The farmer was a potato grower, and Wilf was given all the new varieties to try out in his garden when they first came on the market. This added greatly to his enjoyment in growing potatoes. However, the lifting of heavy sacks of potatoes injured his back so severely that he was off sick for a year, so after that he went to work at the ammunition factory at Glascoed for thirteen years. During his time there he did little vegetable showing because his children were growing up and he found he needed any spare money for them. In any event, children absorb time like sponges, and time is the one asset above all that showmen need.

By 1979 he found his back was so much recovered that he could contemplate going to work outside once more, this time for the County Council in their Highways Department. It was then that he began to show seriously, in large part because of the encouragement of a work-mate, who had shown vegetables successfully all his life. Wilf remembers George Matthews winning prizes when he was a boy, so it was a great treat to talk to him about showing, particularly as George Matthews was one of those men prepared to tell what he knew. Showing 'was the topic every day, very near, when we two got together.'

As well as the garden to the front and side of the house, for about twenty years Wilf has looked after a long thin piece of ground next to the road nearby. It faces south and is therefore 'earlier' than his own garden. The soil is also lighter so is more quickly workable in the spring. The advantage of this is obvious: Wilf can produce the same vegetables for different shows from the two gardens.

Wilf did not show at Abergavenny Show in 1988 because a bout of 'flu in the spring incapacitated him just when he should have been sowing his seed. Such a setback is serious for an exhibitor who must time his gardening almost to the day. The year before, however, he did show at Abergavenny, and had particular success

with his sweet peas, winning the Perpetual Silver Challenge Cup for the second year running. His vegetable 'collection' was adjudged extremely good but he lost the chance of a prize 'on the pointage', that is, he failed to win because he had entered some low point vegetables, namely beetroot, broad beans and cabbage.

To the ordinary gardener, without show experience, the points system is as meaningless as Morse Code to a landlubber. Yet without knowledge of it no showman will get very far. It covers all horticultural produce, but matters particularly for vegetable exhibitors. Most judges at shows, as I have said before, depend on *The Horticultural Show Handbook*, which contains details of the maximum points that may be awarded for every conceivable type of horticultural produce if the show is being judged 'under RHS rules'. Even if the show is not specifically under RHS rules, judges will often rely on them informally. In close competition, they use the information in the Handbook to assess the maximum points they can award for, say, uniformity, size and condition (as well as a number of variables, depending on the vegetable, such as solidity in leeks, fullness of pods in peas, and shallowness of the 'eyes' in potatoes). The RHS recognizes that some vegetables are harder to grow well

The day before the show on 29 July, Harry Clarke cuts through a beetroot to check that there are no white rings.

than others; for example, there is an obvious disparity between the skill needed to grow good salad onions and good cauliflowers. That is why the maximum points that a judge can award for a meritorious (the common malapropism for this amongst showmen is 'emeritus') salad onion is five whereas for a meritorious cauliflower it is twenty. No vegetable can receive more than twenty. In a class of cauliflowers, say, the judge may be able to judge the exhibits without needing to add up the points they score in three categories (condition ten, solidity six, uniformity four) but in a close-fought class it will be necessary to do so.

Counting points is absolutely essential when he is judging a 'collection' of vegetables, where an exhibitor may have anything up to eight different kinds of vegetable displayed. Not only does the judge need to use the points system in order to be sure that he has been fair in his decision, but exhibitors like him to write down the points awarded so that they can see how he reached his decision. The collection is far and away the most prestigious vegetable class, and judges approach the judging of it with enormous circumspection – and not a little trepidation.

Of course, if you are not aware of the pointing system, or you do not have sufficient vegetables to put in all 'twenty pointers', you are at a distinct disadvantage. For, however good your cabbages are, they can never earn more than fifteen points, whereas good, but not first-class, onions might well receive sixteen. Experienced exhibitors understand this perfectly well but nowhere will you see it referred to in show schedules. Showmen find this out only by talking to other showmen, a state of affairs which inevitably leads to disappointment and disillusionment amongst novices, and which should be a matter of shame to flower show committees.

Wilf's difficulties with the 'collection' in 1987 did not arise out of ignorance, of course. He knew perfectly well about the points system; he just found himself without enough good quality twenty-point vegetables, something which can happen to anyone. The vegetable 'collections' at shows tax exhibitors' resources enormously, and the best-organized gardener can find himself without the 'stuff' to show.

For those, and there are some, who believe the range of vegetables grown for show is too traditional, centred as it is round parsnips, onions, carrots and potatoes, the points system has one great disadvantage. As long as maximum points are awarded to those vegetables, (together with celery, leeks and peas) and as long as vegetable 'collections' attract the most prize money and prestige, the growing of these will always absorb most of exhibitors' energies.

Apart from sweet peas and dahlias, Wilf probably enjoys growing potatoes as much as anything. There are

four classes at Abergavenny: white, kidney (five); white, round (five); coloured, kidney (five); and coloured, round (five). That is a good selection for a local show: many shows have dropped down to just two classes, white and coloured. The varieties he was showing in 1989 for the four classes were respectively 'Pentland Dell', 'Croft', 'Catriona' and 'Cara'.

Unlike the average gardener, who buys his potato 'seed' each year to prevent the build-up of diseases, particularly virus and scab, in the stock, Wilf saves his 'seed' from year to year. He does, however, also try one or two new varieties each year. To prevent deterioration, he grows them alternately in the garden and in his allotment nearby. As the soil is alkaline, his main headache is to prevent the fungus disease 'common scab' forming on the skins of the potatoes. Scab makes little difference to the cook but ruins a potential exhibition potato, and it is most prevalent in alkaline soils (particularly if the potatoes come in contact with stones in the soil), and in hot dry summers.

Each exhibitor seems to swear by a different remedy. Wilf finds sedge peat does not work, so prefers to lay a layer of well-rotted compost or mushroom compost along the trench and above the seed potatoes, so that the offspring tubers do not touch the soil at all. In 1989, he rang the changes, experimenting with decaying grass-clippings from the churchyard which he looks after.

Soil does not feature, either, in the growing of his long carrots (Sutton's 'New Red Intermediate'), the seed of which is sown straight into a soil-less mixture which has been put in 2′6″ tall drainpipes or oil drums. First he fills the container with a mixture of peat and sand; then he bores holes down to the bottom and fills these with a mélange of peat, sand, 'Seagold' seaweed manure, bonemeal and Bromophos (a granular soil insecticide which prevents carrot fly infestation). There is no farmyard manure, which might encourage the carrots to fork. This light, porous mixture suits the carrot very well but needs a great deal of water in dry weather: if the soil dries out, the carrots will split.

He also grows stump-rooted ('shorthorn') carrots called 'Chantenay Red-Cored'; 'Dok Elgon' summer-maturing cauliflower; 'Shamrock Big Apple' cabbage; 'Windsor Longpod' broad beans; 'Tender and True' parsnips; Sutton's 'Achievement' runner beans; 'Crimson Globe' or 'Boltardy' globe beetroot; 'Prizetaker' leeks; 'Kelsae' onions; and 'Showmaster' onion sets from Marshalls. In 1989 he grew his peas, 'Show Perfection', on the cordon system in the same way as he grows his sweet peas. He cleaves to the old, tried and tested varieties which he acquires from the big mail-order seed firms.

A gardener of immense experience, Wilf is, interestingly, not a devotee of 'double-digging', the back-breaking task often proclaimed by people as their credential to be *bona fide* exhibitors. Although the soil in his garden is heavy, he does not double-dig except where he will plant his onions and, even there, he is not entirely convinced of the efficacy of it. After all, as he points out, onion roots do not go down more than nine inches.

In the matter of feeding Wilf's views are mainstream: plenty of farmyard manure and bonemeal in the autumn, the general fertilizer 'Growmore' ten days before sowing, and 'Phostrogen' as a liquid feed regularly every ten days during the summer.

Wilf takes enormous trouble over the preparation of his vegetables for show. He digs the potatoes up very carefully, and immediately wraps them individually in newspaper so that the skins are not damaged. This is particularly important when preparing for an early show like Abergavenny, because the skins of maincrop varieties have not yet hardened by the end of July. The newspaper also prevents 'greening', which develops very quickly if the stem tubers are left exposed to the air. He takes the tubers into the kitchen and first soaks them in clean cold water to remove most of the soil. He then washes them in the lather of an ordinary washing soap, using a soft sponge. After a rinse in clean cold water, he removes any brown marks very gently with a soft cloth and rubs and dries the potato. Getting five to match, he says, is the biggest problem. He can wash twenty or thirty potatoes before he gets the five he wants. He can

get them nearly right sometimes but perhaps one has a deeper eye or a brown mark where it comes off the haulm. 'You've got to take all that into consideration.'

In comparison, carrots are quite easy. To begin with, unlike potatoes, they can be matched before they come out of the soil. It is usually possible to gauge by the circumference of the tops whether they are of a comparable size. Getting them out of the ground does require patience, it is true. Wilf removes about two inches of compost from around the crown of the carrot so that he can pour copious quantities of water round it. He usually leaves the water to soak in for several hours before attempting to remove it and, if it does not come out easily, he will add more water and settle down to wait. After a decent interval has elapsed, he takes the foliage in one hand and continues to add water as he eases the carrot out. If any other method is adopted there is always the chance that some of the thread-like 'whip', so prized by exhibitors, will break off.

Once the carrots are removed from the ground, however, they need only be checked for marks on the roots. They are washed in clean water, using a sponge; Wilf moves the sponge round and round the carrot rather than from top to bottom. This is because there are often tiny lateral roots which, if they get under the sponge, can mark the carrot all the way down. Any small mark will only appear when the carrot is dry.

Parsnips are chosen and cleaned in the same way. The same goes for beetroot, but the emphasis is on cleaning them without breaking the taproot, because it will 'bleed'. In order to see that his beetroot do not have white rings, Wilf will emulate the judge and cut one open beforehand. It is not a complete safeguard, however: as Wilf has found in the past, beetroot can be pulled one day and be uniformly purple-red inside, yet develop white rings by the next. He tries to prevent this by watering his beetroot with a saline solution, although never very close to the roots because salt can burn them. As beetroot is a seaside plant there is much sense in it. Some showmen, apparently, will make up a solution and soak the beetroot in it overnight before the show, but Wilf thinks this a last-ditch expedient and not as effective as watering with salty water while the beet is growing. Incidentally, beet are subject to damage by the same common scab that affects potatoes, so roots must be chosen which are not only young and tender, and the size of a tennis ball, but with unblemished skins as well.

Some vegetables can be used for more than one show. Wilf has won three first prizes with the same three carrots at three shows held on consecutive days. In order to do so, he wrapped them in a damp cloth the moment the

Wilf Mayo 'rising' his potatoes. He wraps them immediately in newspaper to prevent them from greening.

first show was over to keep them from drying out before the next. He says that they will keep for three to four days but not as long as a week.

According to Wilf, the world is divided into exhibitors who will tell you if you are making a mistake and those who will not, of which the latter are the more numerous. The first year he went to Abergavenny Show, for some reason, which he cannot explain, he thought that he needed to put six instead of five potatoes on each dish. He was taken aside by another exhibitor, a Mr Hall, who said, 'There's something wrong with these potatoes,' to which Wilf replied, 'They're as good as yours'. It says something for Mr Hall's good nature that he still went on to say that Wilf had one too many potatoes on each plate. Wilf thanked him, removed a potato from each of his dishes and succeeded in taking first prize from Mr Hall in every potato class. This incident plainly had an effect on Wilf, because not only did he become friendly with Mr Hall but it stiffened his resolve to pass on useful tips to any novice exhibitor.

He worries that the classic vegetables are no longer attracting the numbers of exhibitors that they were. This is of course a subjective judgement but might well be borne out by the show committee. The 'easy' vegetables

Wilf 'rises' a carrot from the soil-less compost in a drainpipe. The variety is Sutton's 'New Red Intermediate'.

such as beetroot or pickling shallots, which require no special treatment, may get twelve or fifteen entries, but large onions, which will need enormous amounts of preparation and care, may attract only a couple of entries each year.

Wilf is firmly of the opinion (and I have heard this view expressed also by experienced judges) that the size of the vegetable makes little or no difference to its taste, providing it has been grown quickly and well. He maintains this even for parsnips and carrots, and believes that show peas actually taste sweeter because they have been fed and watered with great care. Certainly a good judge can distinguish between large and tender and large and coarse, and it is inevitable that there will be an emphasis on size when large good vegetables are so much harder to grow than small ones.

Wilf can be a little dismissive of the modern judge, exhibiting the scepticism practical men feel for book-learning. 'Years ago the judge was actually a vegetable grower himself. Nowadays you get judges who go to college and they never grow any vegetables so how do they know what a perfect specimen is? I showed at . . . two years ago and I put three beautiful carrots in the show. Any other show I'd have taken first prize. But he cut the carrot in half. Well, that's the first time I'd ever known a carrot being cut in a show. Cut a beetroot, yes, but not a carrot. . . He threw me out because the core was too thick in the carrot!' The last sentence was uttered in a tone of disbelief.

Just over the hill from Llanvetherine is the small village of Llanvapley. Here lives Ken Bevan, a retired dragline operator who has had much success in local shows in recent years. He is friendly, self-confident and likeable, with a weakness for innocent boasting. He is one of the most reflective and adventurous showmen that I have met, always thinking about how he might improve his cultivation techniques and show preparation. He enjoys winning and takes pride in the fact that he does well without enjoying particular advantages.

Except, that is, access to a larger than average plot of land. His own garden is not big but, in exchange for keeping the Old Rectory garden in order, he has half of the large vegetable garden for his own use. This is very useful for a man who likes to grow up to ten potato varieties. The soil is a heavy loam. Perhaps because he has so much garden to look after, and, anyway, was recovering from a hernia operation in 1989, he is not as neat and tidy a gardener as Wilf. However, his methods are effective.

Ken was born on a farm in Breconshire, but gave up farming after a bad tractor accident in 1947. After he recovered, he went to work for a civil engineering firm, continuing in the work until he retired as general foreman in 1987. He and his wife Nancy have lived in Llanvapley since the late 60s. He maintains that gardening is in the blood, for it 'is only just farming on a smaller scale'.

In 1984 a friend encouraged him to enter the vegetable section at Abergavenny Show. He admits that he did not have a clue about presentation. After the judging was over he sent his son John to see how he had fared, while he stayed loitering amongst the flower exhibits. He told him, 'If we haven't got nothing, we'll leave the blooming things there.' John came running back saying, 'Dad, Dad, you've won the flipping lot.' Ken did not believe him until he had seen for himself the first prize cards for onions and carrots. It particularly pleased him to have beaten local professional gardeners. Ken proved that it is possible to win without any idea of the proper techniques of showing.

Ken did not enter the show the following year but went to see what he would have been up against: 'I could have walked away with it' [the cup]. This was no idle boast, for the following year, 1986, he won the Perpetual Challenge Cup for most points in the vegetable section and a Diploma of Excellence for the best exhibit, namely the vegetable 'collection', and, in 1988, he was one point short of winning the cup again.

His great loves are the classically difficult vegetables, which he grows with due regard for scientific discoveries. He buys his potatoes from a specialist Scottish firm, ordering four varieties for the potato classes and four

reserves. He told me, in a suitably shocked tone, that some cost forty pence a tuber. His first choices in 1989 were 'Baillie', a round, white potato; 'Catriona', long, purple-eyed; 'Penta', round, pink-eyed; and 'Pentland Dell', long and white. He also had 'Ulster Sceptre', long, white; 'Vanessa', long, red; 'Cara', round, pink-eyed; and 'Anta', long, pink.

Ken is very subtle and does not grow those potato varieties which are described as 'oval'. This is because they have a proportion of round as well as kidney-shaped potatoes and therefore more roots must be dug to get the right amount of tubers for the dishes. He does not bother with 'Homeguard', for example, which is described as 'round, oval, white'.

Unlike Wilf Mayo, Ken swears by sedge peat as his talisman against scab. In his potato trenches he first puts well-rotted farmyard manure (no one has any difficulty finding it in this agricultural area), covers that with rotted grass clippings and puts peat on top. He lays the seed potatoes in the trench and covers them in peat, finishing off with soil. Like Wilf, he tends to save his seed from year to year, but says that unless you know how to do it there is no point in saving potato 'seed'. The method he employs is this: he plants the 'seed' late in the year, well after the conventional time which is April, in not very good ground, and 'rises' them late. He then only keeps the small tubers, under the size of an average hen egg.

He does not grow his parsnips and carrots in drainpipes (maintaining that they dry out too quickly in summer and suffer too much from fluctuations in temperature) but prefers to bore deep holes in prepared ground, into which he puts a mixture of one part soil, one part peat and one part sand (he uses builder's sand because sharp sand is too expensive for him), two ounces of 'Seagold', and two ounces of superphosphate per bushel. Carrots are treated similarly and Ken is very proud of the fact that he once grew a carrot which, with whip, was 6′ 10½″ long, *and* he says he left about a foot of it in the ground. Apparently, only eighteen inches or so actually resembled a carrot.

The growing of onions gives him enormous pleasure. He grows every conceivable kind: pickling shallots, large shallots, Japanese onions (for which there is a class at Abergavenny Show) and the large 'Kelsae' onions. The largest of these that he has succeeded in growing was six and a quarter pounds at a time when the world record was still under eight pounds, which is very creditable for a man who does not go as far as installing growing lights in the greenhouse or other techniques favoured by the national exhibitors. He does, however, grow his large onions under polythene covers in a special double raised

Wilf's vegetable garden with his sweet peas, grown 'on the cordon', in the background.

'deep bed', which can be reached from a path which goes down the middle. The soil is raised up and retained by wooden boards to ensure good drainage and is double-dug every three years. (Unlike other crops, which are rotated, onions can be grown on the same land for years unless there are disease problems.) Over the beds is a wooden frame, open on the top but with clear polythene sheeting hanging down the sides. This worked well in 1989 because the shelter did not get too hot. Ken toyed with the idea of putting down the new black-and-white polythene sheeting, which has become so popular with serious showmen. It is placed black side down to discourage weeds, while the white side reflects more light on to the onions. I suspect it will not be long before he acquires some, for he is an enterprising gardener.

His big 'Kelsae' onions are never ripe for the Abergavenny Show, but he pulls some nevertheless. The Japanese onions, sown the summer before, are ready, of course, because they mature in early summer; they, like the 'Hâtive de Niort' shallots, are designed to bridge the gap until this year's crop is ready.

It is a pleasure to see the peas 'Show Perfection' that Ken grows on the 'cordon' system, as if they were sweet peas. It is wasteful of space and time-consuming, for the gardener must be for ever pinching out the tendrils and sideshoots, but it is highly desirable if they are to be exhibited. This is the pursuit of excellence in its purest form. The show ideal is a pod filled, without gaps, with thirteen peas. Ken takes infinite care with them when picking the ones for show, holding them up to the light so that he can count the peas inside, then cutting those he wants one and a half inches from the pod with a pair of sharp scissors. As with fruit and succulent plants, it is important to leave the 'bloom' on the peapods, so Ken takes with him an empty ice box into which he gently lowers the peas. Unlike many gardeners, who use metal sweet pea rings for holding the pea stems to the canes, Ken uses his wife's laddered stockings, which he cuts into short lengths. He finds them excellent because they are flexible and expand slightly as the pea stems grow.

In 1989 he was anxious that his hernia operation the winter before might have made him too late in sowing his seeds. Certainly it was March before he really got going. Fortunately he believes that it is possible to start some plants, such as parsnips, too early (the received wisdom is that they should be sown in late February or early March). He is of the opinion that seedlings are like the young of farm animals. If they get a check from cold weather or lack of food just after they are taken away from their mothers they never do very well, and cold weather checks seedling parsnips so that they never quite recover: 'If he's skinted when he's small, he'll never come the same.' In 1989 he grew for the first time the quicker-maturing, smooth-skinned, very long-rooted hybrid parsnip from Thompson and Morgan called 'Gladiator', and was not unduly worried that he did not sow it until the first week in April.

Like Wilf, Ken takes great care over picking and preparing his 'stuff', lifting and drying his onions and shallots well in advance and tying the necks. There are two ways of doing this: either cutting the neck back to about three inches and wrapping it very tightly with raffia so that it looks thin, or folding a longer neck over and wrapping it tightly on itself. He uses damp cloths to keep the carrots and parsnips fresh once lifted, and carefully trims them of any fine lateral roots; straightens any bent runner beans by wrapping them in a damp cloth attached to a thin lath; and takes a ruler to his marrows to find a well-matched pair.

Ken enters several shows (Abergavenny, Cwmyoy, Cross Ash, Llanvapley) in the course of the summer, in 1988 and 1989 straying as far as the very large Gower Show near Swansea. He has a certain hankering to enter the 'Kelsae' onion competition held each year at Harrogate, where the first prize is £750 (the first prize for the vegetable 'collection' at Abergavenny is £10), but he recognizes that this may be rather ambitious at his age. If he were a little younger and better placed he might have become a national exhibitor. As it is, he enjoys the prestige which goes with being a successful local exhibitor.

As reflective as Ken Bevan in his own way is Harry Clarke, who gardens in rather different circumstances in Abergavenny. His end-of-terrace house has a garden only 30 feet by 75 feet, yet it is not only very gay with hanging baskets and annuals in summer, but also extremely productive as a vegetable garden. Unlike Ken, who undoubtedly grows to show, Harry has an eye all the time to what is required in the kitchen.

Harry was born not far away in the village of Grosmont, on the edge of the Black Mountains, the son of a painter and decorator. He freely admits that he used to find gardening time-consuming and a bore, but circumstances compelled him to keep a garden in order, and he gradually began to see the point of it all. He is a softly-spoken man but with decided views, independent-minded, self-respecting and with a sense of humour. (My assumption that showmen would be too self-absorbed and intense to laugh at themselves did not long survive my meetings with them.)

When Harry left school he spent a few years on a farm before joining the navy during the war. When the war ended, he took to lorry-driving because he preferred not to have a boss looking over his shoulder. Since 1977, he has lived in Abergavenny, working at the telephone exchange as a supervisor and finishing as officer-in-charge. He retired in 1986.

His showing ambition was fired by men he knew who boasted of their achievements at shows. Harry's irritation at this bragging prompted him to chance his own arm in about 1981. At his first attempt at Abergavenny Show he won some of the vegetable classes and was encouraged to continue. Abergavenny is his nearest show, but he also shows in some years at Llangattock Crickhowell, Gilwern and the Abergavenny Horticultural Society's show in early September.

His favourite vegetables are onions, leeks, parsnips, celery and carrots, because he likes the look of them. He does not think much of lettuce and cabbage, but that may be because there is so little, comparatively, to their cultivation. He does grow cauliflower for the vegetable 'collection', but it is rare that he has any ready at the right moment; in such a restricted space it is impossible to stagger planting for such large vegetables. After all, the time it will take for cauliflowers to mature is hard to anticipate, unlike peas, for example, which nearly always take sixteen to seventeen weeks from the time of sowing to harvest.

Like Wilf, Harry does not do a lot of double-digging and is not convinced that he gets any better results if he does. (No one could ever accuse these chaps of being lazy; if they thought double-digging really made a difference they would not shrink from the work involved – which is considerable.) He does, however, dig in plenty of four-year-old farmyard manure. However, unlike

Wilf, Harry has a very light sandy soil overlying river gravel, which dries quickly in summer but is workable at all times of the year. 'The wife comes in handy for watering.'

Harry grows everything from seed or cuttings, including the many occupants of the hanging baskets. He even saves the bulbils from leeks, that is the little 'pips' which grow from the leek seedheads if the leeks are potted up and left to grow on for a second year. He usually saves some of his own onion seed, too, but is not quite confident enough to rely on it entirely, and so buys 'Kelsae' seed as well. 'Kelsae' is probably the most popular exhibitor's onion to be grown from seed; Harry likes it as much for its flagon, not-too-bulbous shape as for its legendary size and weight.

True to time-honoured tradition, Harry sows his onions on Christmas Day (a practice developed by gardeners as an excuse to get out of the washing-up), 'or Christmas Eve if the mood takes me', for onions need a long growing season if they are to reach a respectable size. He puts them in gentle heat, as onions will not germinate easily above 18°C (65°F). He pricks them out at the 'loop' stage into individual pots and grows them on in gentler heat, eventually putting them into the cold greenhouse to harden them off before he plants them out in mid-April.

The appeal of the onion is a strange but undoubtedly potent one. It really does have little to do with its culinary virtues. Although the exhibitor will tell you that a huge onion is perfectly useful because it can be cut in half and kept in the fridge, it is the challenge of growing it well which appeals. Like Ken Bevan, Harry grows his onions under cover, in this instance a shelter made mainly from the sides of his wife's old wooden budgerigar aviary. The half-inch wire netting is covered in durable polythene. He keeps one end of it open in hot weather.

Working under cover poses a problem for Harry but he is lucky to have such an amiable wife. His wife, Fay, has, apparently, spent many a half-hour weeding the onions. Harry says she is a bit more stable on her feet than he is and 'one knock on an onion at any stage of its growth and that onion's finished.'

Harry is at one with Ken Bevan on the matter of whether drainpipes are necessary for growing root vegetables. He prefers to bore 4' 6" inch holes in the ground with an iron bar for the parsnips. He is convinced that this reduces the need for watering, a real consideration on his light soil. The longest parsnip that he measured in 1988 was exactly 4'6" long, so the root had managed to reach to the bottom of the hole. He trickles a few granules of 'Growmore' into the hole, when he has bored it, so that the taproot has something to feed on should it reach the bottom. These touches may not make much difference but they are psychologically important.

LEFT Ken Bevan's 'Kelsae' onions trimmed and tied with raffia. As the show is so early these are still rather white.

RIGHT Ken straightens his runner beans using a damp cloth and thin wooden lath.

Harry's parsnip and carrot mix was gleaned recently from *Garden News*. It is as follows: three parts soil (unlike Wilf's which contains no soil at all), one part Irish moss peat, two parts sand, put through a quarter-inch mesh; to each bushel of mixture is added two ounces of coarse bonemeal, two ounces of superphosphate, four ounces of 'Seagold', two ounces of sulphate of potash and a generous sprinkling of 'Bromophos' mixed thoroughly.

A bushel measures eight gallons 'dry' but, as Harry says, it is easier to think of it as the volume of the average garden wheelbarrow: 'I've got my wheelbarrow marked with a pencil line.' In 1989 Harry had great difficulty finding dry loam, so instead he began using a mixture of a proprietary peat-based compost as well as a John Innes No. 1 compost to which he added two tablespoons full of 'Phostrogen'.

Harry 'chits' his parsnip seed before he sows it at the end of February; he has discovered, by trial and error, that it takes only about eight days for the seed to germinate on moist kitchen roll in a tray in the heated greenhouse (as opposed to almost five weeks outside in February). In 1989 Harry found that the first batch germinated so quickly that, before he noticed, they had one and a half inch long roots which were already beginning to curl round. At that stage he threw them out, thinking already that he would not get the straight roots that he requires. Such is his attention to detail.

It may be that he is haunted by an experience he had when he first began to grow for show. He knew he was supposed to grow carrots in tubs but he did not know how to go about it. He filled them with compost, but, as it was early in the year, he sowed the carrots in the greenhouse in the centres of lavatory paper rolls. They germinated well but what he did not realize was that the taproot of the seed had gone down to the very bottom. When he planted them out in the tubs, the cardboard rolls rotted away but the taproots had curled up. So the carrots grew quite happily until he lifted them but they were quite matted.

He answers small advertisements in *Garden News* to get his blanched leek 'pips'. As he is buying from other exhibitors he hopes that what he receives is a proven strain. The advertisements make claims that the leeks have been winners in particular shows, but this method of buying is still something of a lottery. 'I suppose you've got a tendency to believe them', he says with touching faith in the veracity of other exhibitors. He pays about £1.50 for ten bulbils.

One of the most extraordinary sights in a showman's garden is the leek bed, with its line of broad grey-green flag leaves growing out of grey drainpipes. The emphasis in blanched leek showing is on producing large plants with a good length of 'blanch', that is, white edible stem, and the way to do this is to exclude the light completely. Harry aims for a two-foot length of blanch but he rarely achieves it. (Long leeks should not be confused with 'pot' leeks; these are grown in pots or in trenches and the blanch must be *exactly* six inches, but with as large a diameter as is humanly possible.)

Although they are hardy, Harry starts his leeks off in the heated greenhouse as 'pips' in November, potting them up individually when they are the thickness of a 'biro cartridge tube' in about January. This is when he puts one-inch diameter pipes over them to encourage them from early days to grow upwards and to begin to blanch. When he plants them out into the garden in April, he removes the inch pipes, and puts over two-and-three-quarter-inch diameter pipes, cut into twelve to fourteen-inch lengths, instead and, on top of those, four to five-inch diameter downpipes. When the leaves have grown up enough to clear the outer pipe, he brings the inner pipe up and fills the space between the two pipes with peat. When the peat is put between the pipes, the inner one rests on the peat. That means it can easily and slowly be pulled up as the leek grows. The advantages of peat are that it excludes light, it keeps the stems clean, and it is spongey, so it does not stop the expansion of the leek. He is very careful not to overfeed his leeks with nitrogen, lest they split or become soft.

Harry can tell the length of the blanch by the height of the pipe and the leeks he chooses to dig up for show must be uniform in girth. His guide to their thickness is the width of the 'flags', or leaves. Having decided which he will dig up, he levers up the roots carefully with a fork and removes the dirt from the 'beard', so that the outer collar can slip down easily, followed by the inner pipe.

He takes infinite care over the washing of the leek, dipping it in clean water and removing all the dirt with a sponge. Encased as it has been for months, the leek is snow-white beneath the thick green flags: for men like Harry it is an object of beauty and justifiable pride. If there is a split or blemish in the outer layer he will remove that layer. Once that is done, the 'beard' of roots must be cleaned of sticking soil and then 'combed' using a knitting needle. Harry is most particular about this. Once it is clean and dry, Harry will tie the leek 'flags'. He starts at the blanch end and ties them at six-inch intervals. They will then stand upright on the back board of his vegetable 'collection'.

Perhaps not so strangely, taking into account geographical proximity, Harry obtains his runner bean seed from the same man as Ken does – 'Taffy' Stenner from Bridgend. 'They're rather a slender bean. They don't come terribly long. When I dealt with him for the first time . . . he said, "I'll tell you now, if you're looking for a twenty-inch bean don't come to me. But if you want eighteen-inch beans, you'll have as many as you want." I think some judges like a bean to be a bit on the wide side but I've found, really, across the board, that the slender bean seems to take more prizes.' Ken says the beans are 'as straight as gunbarrels'.

In the past, Harry has grown eleven strains of potato, which seems rather extraordinary and may have something to do with the fact that he used to drive potato lorries from Wales to East Anglia but, in 1989, he cut down to five. Because he is growing for the kitchen as well he steers clear of 'Catriona', favoured by the others, because it does not cook well. In 1989 his choice was 'Penta' (round, pink-eyed), 'Kirsty' (white, round/oval), 'Ulster Sceptre' (oval, white), 'Alhambra' (red, round) and 'Pentland Javelin' (round/oval, white). Because he has so little ground he plants early potatoes and the maincrop varieties at the same time. As the maincrop types take longer to mature, he must do this if there is not

Harry washing 'Gladiator' parsnips and his own strain of leeks.

to be left a period of time when he has none ready to eat.

His scab remedy is different again from that employed by Ken or Wilf, leaving one to conjecture whether there are in fact as many scab remedies as there are exhibitors. He likes to use weathered chimney soot, if he can get it. If he cannot (and it is harder, now that boilers are oil-fired, to get pure coal soot from the chimney sweep) he uses moss peat. He avoids the coarser sedge peat favoured by Ken because he thinks it causes black pieces to stick stubbornly to the potatoes; in his opinion, in the process of removing these, the skin may also come off. He never feeds his potatoes with fertilizer but prefers to put them on top of a bed of well-rotted farmyard manure, because there is general agreement that potatoes grown in a moist soil are more resistant to scab.

He grows peas by the cordon method, despite the fact that he does not get nearly as many peas, as each plant must be such a distance (six to nine inches) apart. He cuts the stalks with scissors and lays the pods carefully on tissues after he has picked them, to preserve the 'bloom'. He has been told that nettle leaves are even better because the peas can rest on the stinging hairs. I should not be surprised to hear that he had tried this, because it is the minutiae of growing and show preparation which he seems to enjoy so much.

One of the hardest vegetables to grow well is celery; it is often shunned by showmen because it can rot in the middle overnight and is very prone to slug damage. It also requires a great deal of water. Harry grows the attractive pink-tinged variety, 'Ideal', on the flat, rather than in trenches, to avoid the possibility of soil getting inside the bunch, but it means he must water well. At planting out time, he ties the stems together loosely to encourage them to grow upright, for the inner ones are otherwise inclined to curl. About two months before the show, when the plants are twelve to fourteen inches high, he starts to blanch the sticks by wrapping round them bituminous felt (the kind used for damp-proofing houses) and tying it together. This is done quite loosely so that air can get to the heart of the plant. He is very careful not to dose the celery with a feed too high in nitrogen, lest he encourage heart rot. The celery is harvested close to show-time, so that it looks fresh and crisp; the roots are trimmed off at the base and the plants then wrapped carefully in cloth, for the stems are brittle. Celery has a 'back' and a 'front' and is staged presenting its more attractive side.

Such a perfectionist is Harry that he professes himself never satisfied with what he has put in a show. And he thinks hard about what the judges are looking for when he selects his vegetables. For example, he tries to put all twenty-point vegetables in the 'collection', which is why he is prepared to pull leeks for the Abergavenny Show when they are not as mature as they would be later on and there is no individual class for them. He loves arranging

A snow-white 'blanch' after months incarcerated in two widths of drainpipe.

the vegetable 'collection': 'I think a well-staged "collection" of good grown stuff is a spectacle on its own. . . You've got a variety of vegetables there to look at. And if it's staged tidy, you can see that one will complement the others'.

To many people the judging of vegetables seems rather artificial because horticultural judges (unlike cookery and wine judges) do not taste anything. And there is little doubt that, because amateurs can buy seed of commercially attractive tomatoes such as 'Moneymaker', the winning tomatoes may not actually taste of very much. An excellently flavoured tomato like 'Gardener's Delight', on the other hand, rarely wins prizes at shows because it is too small.

Harry would agree that show carrots are not enormously useful in cooking because so little is edible and they tend to get rather hard as the season progresses; he thinks onions are also rather too large, although they only do well in shows if they are firm and succulent. However he would not pick broad beans, peas or tomatoes any earlier for the kitchen. Nor are large leeks or celery unappetizing, and both beetroot and potatoes lose points if they are very big. 'There's very little that you could say was just good for show work: I think you can use all of it. I grow for show and for the kitchen. It's just,' (with a laugh), 'the shows win when they're on.'

A few years ago he was 'rising' his four sets of potatoes for a show. He had cleaned the first lot and put them on a tray in the lean-to next to the kitchen. When he had dug the rest he could not find the first set, and after a certain amount of storming about, he found that they had ended up in the saucepan. 'I was complimented on cleaning them nicely for her.'

Harry believes that there is an advantage in knowing the individual likes of judges which only comes with great experience of local shows, just as lawyers believe that it helps to know the individual characteristics, even foibles, of the judge in front of whom they are appearing. Some horticultural judges, for example, favour slightly larger potatoes than others. Although he thinks the number of competent judges has fallen, he has never considered judging himself because he does not believe he is properly qualified. He is perhaps put off by the idea of courses and exams such as the National Vegetable Society hold to maintain standards.

He is a great admirer of an old judge who had recently retired from judging at Abergavenny, because he used to come to see his garden, something he thinks judges should do much more. He criticizes judges, too, for being 'too lenient', that is prepared to give a first prize whether the standard is high enough or not. As an accomplished exhibitor he no doubt feels pained if sub-standard produce receives the acclaim of first prize.

Like the others, Harry believes that there is some

cheating in local shows but that the showmen know the guilty men and most do not condone it. He thinks that the judges should be stricter about trimmed cauliflowers, for example, and that the schedule should stipulate that there be at least a four-inch stalk so that the exhibits cannot possibly come from anywhere but the exhibitor's garden. The rules for the show at Abergavenny say that the committee reserve the right to visit the gardens or allotments of exhibitors, a statement which may inhibit cheating.

Ken Bevan also deprecates the small amount of dirty tricks which he thinks goes on at local shows. One year he had a cabbage stolen and he suspects that whoever did it probably put it into another show shortly after. He is contemptuous of those who cheat 'for a couple of quid'. He still feels indignant about the experience of a friend of his, who won first prize with some 'Cara' potatoes at a show one year. A man asked to have 'seed' and they agreed he would take those potatoes on the dish. Shortly afterwards, Ken and his friend went to another local show and found that the man had put the potatoes in as his own.

Wilf Mayo tells a story about entering the vegetable classes in a show some years ago. He had for some time been on the verge of winning the cup from the man who always took it, but had never quite managed to amass enough points. One of the classes he entered was for runner beans, and, like all good exhibitors, he almost neurotically counted and recounted to see that he had the right number – twelve – on the dish. However, when he returned after the judging to see how he had done, he found only eleven beans on the dish and his entry card marked NAS (Not According to Schedule). He looked everywhere but could not find the missing bean. He is convinced that his rival took it because he suspected that, if he won the runner bean class, Wilf would take the cup from him. (Experienced exhibitors can often tell who will win a class as well as any judge, which is why a maverick judge can cause such irritation, even resentment.) In Wilf's experience, however, the prizes are not sufficient to lead any but the really vain and unscrupulous astray.

Abergavenny Show, on 29 July, is too early in the season for truly massive vegetables; the seed onions particularly have not reached full size and are not yet ready to be dried off, so any shown will still be white and may look as if they have been 'skinned', something which judges do not like. Experienced judges, of course, will take the earliness of the show into account. It is sufficiently late on in the growing season amply to show the skill of the exhibitors.

However, as show day in 1989 approached there was consternation amongst the exhibitors because of the prolonged dry and hot summer, which, coming as it did

after an almost rainless winter, had forced the water authority to impose a hosepipe ban in June and July. The cauliflowers belonging to both Harry and Wilf went over some weeks before the show, and Ken's peas were also finished. Even the exhibitors' onions were not as big as usual and Harry's were ripening too fast in the Mediterranean conditions in the onion shelter. The quality of the vegetable 'collections' would therefore depend on the potatoes, leeks, carrots and parsnips, but it looked increasingly likely that exhibitors would have to resort to putting in some eighteen-point vegetables like runner beans in order to make up the six varieties required. Wilf had had a difficult season, with hoards of pollen beetle infesting his much-favoured sweet peas, and drought affecting his onions and potatoes. Ken wondered how he would fare, for he did not yet feel fully recovered from his operation. Only Harry seemed irrepressibly, if quietly, optimistic.

At Abergavenny Show, staging in the Horticultural

TOP LEFT Ken stages his 'Enorma' runner beans.

LEFT Wilf's beautifully uniform and unblemished 'Pentland Dell' win the 'Potatoes, white (5 kidney) named' class. Take no notice of the misleading prize card, put down in error, no doubt, by a busy steward. Wilf also won the 'white, 5 round' class.

RIGHT All four horticultural judges – Mr Holland, Mr Jones, Mr Evans and Mr Ruffell – consult judiciously to find the best matched pair of marrows.

Marquee is done either between four and ten o'clock on Friday evening or early on Saturday, because judging starts promptly at nine o'clock in the morning. As in many shows, the exhibitors must provide all their own vases, boxes and dishes. Only one exhibit is allowed per exhibitor in each class.

The size of the vegetable 'collection' is stipulated in the show schedule and may differ from show to show. At Abergavenny, six distinct kinds are called for with a maximum table frontage of 4′6″, but there is no guidance as to how to stage them. Most exhibitors have made their own 'collection' boards, because the frontage measurement is constant from year to year. The convention is that there should be either a sloping or perpendicular back board, covered in black material, and a black cloth to cover the table in front as well. If cauliflowers are being exhibited they will have their leaves removed and be fastened to the board in a triangle, surrounded with parsley. Celery and leeks are both tied in the shape of a pyramid, with the leek leaves plaited, and attached to the back board by thin string pushed through holes from the back of the board. The onions are often placed on little rings, perhaps short lengths of plastic downpipe, covered with silver foil; these are usually staged in the middle of the bench, flanked by carrots and parsnips, with the 'whip' (the thread-like root) facing the spectator. Beans are staged side by side, and peas in a wheel, with their stalks forming the centre spoke. Potatoes and tomatoes are exhibited on paper plates or dishes.

There are variations on all these themes, depending on the personal preference of the exhibitor: for example, carrots and parsnips are sometimes attached with fine string to the back board, cauliflowers are occasionally displayed on stands. It is impossible to generalize, particularly as some latitude is allowed in these matters at local shows. The Abergavenny Show schedule does not even specify how many of each vegetable should be shown in the vegetable 'collection', although most exhibitors seem to take their cue from the amounts mentioned in the Handbook.

Handsome as the 'collection' board looks, and well as it sets off the vegetables, it can cause problems for judges who find that they cannot easily examine those vegetables attached to the back board. No such difficulty arises with the other 'collections': the five herbs, five salad vegetables and the three 'specimen' vegetables are all staged flat on the bench.

The horticultural entries at Abergavenny in 1989 were slightly up on the previous year which had been wet, but rather less than the two years before that. The Secretary, Mrs Meriel Jones, told the *Abergavenny Chronicle* that they had managed to put on a good show, despite there being fewer floral art and rose entries because of the hot weather. Entries in the vegetable section, however, were better than usual. In the tent, Harry, Ken and Wilf staged their exhibits carefully, unwrapping beans, unpacking plates of onions wedged in cardboard boxes, and arranging the vegetables on the 'collection board' with a skill bordering on artistry. Sadly, the weather defeated Wilf: he had not enough high-scoring vegetables to make up a satisfactory 'collection', and decided in the end to concentrate on individual classes, particularly potatoes and carrots. Harry and Ken (along with six others) entered the 'collection' class (first prize a cup and £10), and took care to cover most of the individual classes as well in order to be in the running for the cup for most points scored in the section and £10.

On the morning of the show the vegetable judges arrived carrying sharp pocket knife, tape measure and inch-diameter ring in their pockets: the inch ring for the pickling shallots, the tape measure to compare the sizes of the partners in a matched pair of marrows and the length of courgettes (ideally four to six inches with the flower still attached), and the knife to cut beetroot in half. Carrots, parsnips and onions would not be cut, of course, while broad beans and peas would have one pod opened, and runner beans one pod snapped, to indicate how young (or old and stringy) they were. These are time-honoured customs and there was, the exhibitors would have been relieved to know, no departure from the norm that day.

Experienced judges, Handbook in hand, are looking for particular general attributes (as described in the Introduction) such as form, colour, uniformity and condition, but are also influenced by other factors, depending on the vegetable. Good French beans, for example, should have straight, tender pods, ideally about ten inches in length (fifteen points maximum). Apart from the size the same applies to runner beans; interestingly only three out of the eighteen possible points are awarded for size, whereas eight are for condition. Like the other beans, broad beans (fifteen), should have a length of stalk attached but, unlike runner beans, the seeds should be obvious, filling the clean and unblemished pods.

Judges tend to dread the globe beetroot (fifteen) class because there are often so many entries. However, many can usually be eliminated because they exhibit white rings when cut, or because they are bigger than the ideal tennis ball size, or have a scabby skin. When all else fails, as they are usually exhibited in threes, uniformity (or lack of it) will decide the issue.

Cabbages (fifteen) must be clean and free of pest damage, well shaped, fresh, and with solid hearts. Long carrots (twenty) must be uniform in length, at least as far as the 'body' of the carrot is concerned, with a good colour, without greening at the top, without side-roots, and without pest damage. There is no doubt that judges

ABOVE Harry's vegetable 'collection' with his own strain of leeks 'like church candles', the pink-tinged 'Ideal' celery, 'Kelsae' onions, 'New Red Intermediate' carrots, 'Stenner strain' runner beans, and 'Gladiator' parsnips. With the exception of the runner beans, all are 'twenty-point' vegetables.

RIGHT Ken and Harry, victors in the vegetable classes.

FAR RIGHT The class for three trimmed onions. The winners are on the top-left; Ken Bevan's are in the middle. Note the balanced presentation of those on the top right.

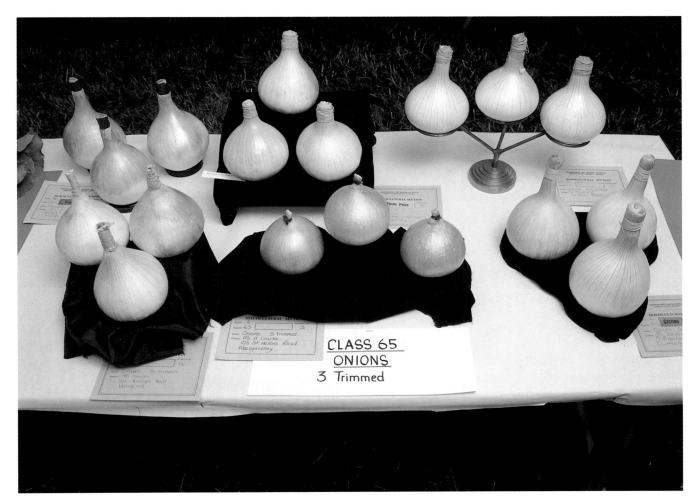

CLASS 65
ONIONS
3 Trimmed

favour those carrots with long 'whips', however useless this attribute may be. But length must be accompanied by quality. Stump-rooted or 'shorthorn' carrots (twenty) find favour if the body of the carrot ends abruptly rather than simply tapering away to nothing, and if it is fat and about six inches from crown to stump. Although easier to grow than long carrots (not grown in drainpipes), these are entitled to receive the same maximum points.

It was a bad year for summer cauliflowers (twenty), but those that there were did well if they had symmetrical, close, white curds, free from staining. Good celery (twenty) has straight stems, a solid heart, a large head of green leaves, and well-blanched, damage-free leaf stalks. Cucumbers (eighteen) are shown in pairs so find favour if they are uniform, straight, young and fresh, with short 'handles' and, if possible, their flowers still attached.

Leeks (twenty) should be solid, as thick as possible, with long shafts and a good blanch – 'like church candles' as Philip Larkin put it. They should be tight-collared with clean skins and no tendency to 'bulbing'. Lettuces (fifteen) do well if they are firm and tender with an intact heart of good colour. Because marrows are easy to grow and prolific, they only warrant a maximum of ten points. They are usually grown as a pair, so uniformity matters, though not as much as condition. They should be young and tender: the judge will put his thumbnail in at the top, near the stalk end, and, if a drop of moisture appears, he knows the marrow is young and fresh. This is important because the same marrow can become a regular attender at shows throughout the summer and early autumn. Onions (twenty) always give judges pause for thought: they should have thin necks and be firm and solid; at autumn shows they must be well-ripened with an intact skin, but should not be excessively 'skinned'. Size accounts for only five points, the same as for condition, form and uniformity. Parsnips are judged in much the same way as carrots; they are also worth a maximum of twenty points. So are peas, which are ideally large and fresh, with thirteen peas inside if possible and the 'bloom' still evident.

Potatoes (twenty) should have shallow 'eyes', fit in the palm of the hand and be free from blemish, with the skin intact. The hardest requirement is that they should be well-matched. Pickling shallots (twelve) should be uniform, preferably under one inch in diameter, round, solid and well-ripened, with thin necks. Ordinary shallots should be the same, but as big as possible. Like shallots, tomatoes (eighteen) cause headaches for judges because there is usually a large entry. Ideally they should be medium-sized (whatever that means), round, ripe without being soft and of a rich colour. Most important, the calyces ('spiders') should be attached, as they are a good indicator of age: the older the tomato, the more the calyx will have curled upwards.

Harry took the first prize in the vegetable 'collection', receiving eighty-eight points altogether, three ahead of his nearest rival. He also gained first for his French beans, third for shallots, second for shorthorn carrots, second for marrows, third for beetroot, second for runner beans, second for three 'specimen' vegetables ('Kelsae' onion, 'Penta' potato and 'Sutton's Favourite' carrot).

Ken was ten points behind Harry in the collection and was unplaced, but had third for his white, round potatoes, second for broad beans, second for shallots, third for shorthorn carrots, second for long carrots, third for cucumbers, second for his 'collection' of herbs, second for cabbage lettuce, third for onions, first for beetroot, first for runner beans, first for Japanese onions, and second for salad vegetables (two lettuce, three tomatoes, six radishes, one cucumber, and six spring onions). One can only guess at how long all those took to prepare.

Wilf did well with his potatoes (thus justifying his faith in the efficacy of lawn mowings, both to conserve moisture and deter scab), taking a first for white kidney potatoes, white round potatoes and coloured round potatoes. He was third, coming just behind Ken, with his long carrots.

Ken won the Welsh Brewers' Perpetual Challenge Cup for the most points scored in the section, and Harry's superlative vegetable 'collection' earned him the Evans Perpetual Challenge Cup and also the Diploma in Horticulture for the best exhibit in the section. Mr John Evans, one of the judges, confided to the *Abergavenny Chronicle* that judging the vegetables had been a difficult task: *'Considering the type of season we have had, the entries are very good and I have given very high marks for the "Collection of Vegetables" which were of a very high standard.'*

The orderly vegetable garden tended by Willie Addison at Maxwelton House.

CHAPTER TWO

DUMFRIES

Dumfries and Lockerbie
Agricultural Society's Annual Show

Dumfriesshire is a county of rounded hills and green valleys, of straggling square-windowed villages and handsome red sandstone, self-respecting market towns. In the past it has sometimes seen bloody internecine strife amongst rough noblemen, the brutal suppression of religious nonconformity, outbreaks of witchcraft, even cholera, and always travellers passing to and fro. These days life is rather calmer: although the travellers still come they are now called tourists, and it is only their buses which are noisy. They pause briefly on the way to the Highlands, which seem so much more Scottish, somehow, but the region that they hurry through bred the most Scottish of all poets, Robert Burns.

To the English eye, accustomed to changes which have altered country life in the last two decades, this part of south-west Scotland seems more traditional, the people less frenetically mobile and holding faster to the old pursuits. There is, not surprisingly, a network of well-supported flower shows in the region around Dumfries. Although most types of flowers are represented at these shows, the greenhouse pot plants are especially notable, not least because they are so often of indifferent quality at local shows.

Why Lowland Scots should be so successful at growing pot plants can only be a matter of conjecture, but I like to think that the long winters, the comparative lack of sunshine, and an annual rainfall of about forty-five inches encourage gardeners to turn for consolation to their greenhouses. Perhaps, too, the presence of several large houses about Dumfries – Drumlanrig, Kirkconnell, Kinharvie, Portrack, Cowhill, Maxwelton – has meant in the past a lively tradition of private service gardening in the area. After all, professional gardeners on large estates have always had to produce good-quality greenhouse plants for display in 'the big hoose'. As in other places, retiring professional gardeners are not now always replaced, but enough remain to influence showing, both as exhibitors and as expert judges, helping to establish as well as maintain higher than average standards of cultivation.

The first show of the calendar for the local pot-plant growers is the Dumfries and Lockerbie Agricultural Society's Annual Open Show, held on the first Friday and Saturday in August in a cattle shed at Park Farm Showfield. Park Farm is only a mile or so from the centre of Dumfries. The show held there is principally an agricultural and livestock one, of course, but it does have a flourishing 'Flowers, Vegetables, Fruit and Floral Art' section, not to mention 'Industrial and Home Arts' (which is the genteel Scottish way of saying handicrafts, cookery, and home-made walking sticks and shepherd's crooks). Although Dumfries is an ancient royal burgh, with a sturdy civic pride evident in the colourful roadside plantings and an immaculately kept railway station, this agricultural and horticultural show indicates that Dumfriesians are still close to the countryside which surrounds them.

The same group of keen pot plant exhibitors could be seen at any one of perhaps half a dozen local shows in the course of the summer: New Abbey, Castle Douglas, Locharbriggs, Moniaive, Moffat, Thornhill and Loreburn Hall in Dumfries. This is because they are serious amateurs, sufficiently interested to spend six or seven weekends in the summer showing flowering pot plants, and possessing enough of these to have flowers in bloom for all that time.

Most competitors (with a greater or lesser degree of self-knowledge) say they show for the fun, but when Agnes Mowat says it you can believe her. She resolutely refuses to take herself too seriously yet she is an avid competitor. Agnes was not bred in Dumfriesshire but comes from Bonchester, near Hawick, and speaks the attractive, if almost impenetrable, dialect of that district.

Agnes is an instinctive gardener of considerable skill and great commitment, growing unusual plants like the black-flowered veratrum in her herbaceous border, and experimenting each year with a variety of annuals which she shows in the cut flower classes at the shows.

Her first love, however, is the large-flowered tuberous-rooted begonia, of which she has about twenty varieties. Her interest in these exotic plants was kindled by an old man she knew in Bonchester, a very successful showman in his time, who was prepared to teach her about the growing and showing of them. He gave her tubers (known in this part of Scotland as 'corms') to start her off. That was in about 1977, but she did not begin to show her begonias until two years later, when she and her husband moved to Dalry near New Galloway and she was persuaded to enter them in the local show to make up the numbers: 'So I took them up and beat the man that always won! And he was not very pleased.' Agnes' three uncles were all professional gardeners and her grandfather used to win prizes at Bonchester village show. As a child she would gather wild flowers, haws, wild strawberries and acorns to make up a 'box', or float flowers on water in soup-plates. Flower shows therefore never held any terrors for her.

The Mowats moved to Terregles, in the flattish farmland outside Dumfries, in 1983 when Agnes' husband, Peter, took early retirement from his job working for the Forestry Commission. The first local shows that she attended were at Kirkcudbright and Castle Douglas, but she now enters most on the local circuit each summer. Her reason for competing in larger shows since she came to Terregles is a desire to pit her skills against more experienced and capable growers. As far as Agnes is concerned, the more competition the better: a sentiment echoed, incidentally, by all the exhibitors I have met – without exception. For a variety of reasons they feel cheated if the class is small or undistinguished. Agnes is enormously respected by the other exhibitors, as much, I suspect, for her kindness and good humour as for her skill in growing begonias.

The begonias in question are not the half-hardy annuals widely grown in bedding schemes, nor even the rhizomatous 'leaf' begonias grown for the colourful markings on their foliage, like *Begonia rex*, but varieties of *B.* × *tuberhybrida*, technically, if rather long-windedly, called 'large-flowered tuberous-rooted begonias'. They have arisen from crosses between *B. boliviensis*, *B. pearcei* and *B. rosaeflora*, and are therefore sub-tropical plants. They are immensely showy in a slightly blowsy way and over the years have shown themselves so amenable to breeding that double flowers can now be had up to nine inches across, if the plants are grown in good conditions. The delicacy of the flower, with its many petals reminiscent of a flamenco dancer's petticoats, is not always matched by subtlety of colour, but growers can choose from dozens of varieties, ranging from the white 'Diana Wynyard' to the vibrant orange 'Tahiti'. Begonias like high humidity, good ventilation, and protection from direct sunlight, which goes a long way to explaining why they grow so well in Scotland. They do, however, require consistent skilled treatment if they are to flourish, hence their relative unpopularity as show flowers. Ordinary gardeners searching round for something to take to support the local show will not alight on these begonias. They need to be grown specially.

Begonias like a period of dormancy or 'rest' in the winter, and usually begin to die down in the late autumn as the days shorten and the nights grow colder. This is the time when Agnes ceases giving them so much water. When the pots are dry, usually in November, they are tilted so that all the old fleshy stems fall out. The old

soil is cleaned off the tubers, a name-label is tied to each one, and they are then put in boxes of dry peat and left somewhere frost-free (in Agnes' case, in the loft) during the winter.

Some time between late February and late March, the tubers are set into growth again by being placed, hollow side up, in boxes of peat, watered, sprayed over daily with a fine spray of water, and kept at a minimum night temperature of 12°C (55°F). The automatic vents open at 21°C (70°F). When the root system is established and leaf growth has begun, the tubers are potted up into soilless potting compost. Peter does the mixing of this compost in a small concrete mixer, using six buckets of peat to two of sand and adding a packet of 'Chempak' potting fertilizer to each bushel.

The begonias are grown as either single-stemmed plants to produce one very large flower (in which case all other stems are removed), or multi-stemmed plants to make a large head of flowers, in which case at least three stems are allowed to grow up. The single-stemmed plants are used for the so-called begonia 'boards' – that is, they are treated like specimen roses – their flower heads being mounted on sloping black boards with the stems in water. The tubers, from which these are grown, are usually two years old. Begonia 'boards' are only found at shows where keen begonia growers exhibit.

The multi-stemmed plants, on the other hand, are derived from older tubers, sometimes as much as ten or fifteen years old, and can be the size of a soup-plate; they are preserved until such a time as they have lost their vigour and no longer produce many sturdy stems. These tubers get larger every year and are almost like old friends to begonia exhibitors; they refer to the age of the 'corms' as if they were the finest malt whiskies. When I asked Agnes how old a seven-inch wide tuber of 'Tahiti' was, she replied, with understandable pride: 'Oh, by ginge. It'll be away in the teens.' Agnes puts the date of acquisition or propagation on the label and also whether it has won a cup for her.

Depending on the date when the tubers are started into growth, but usually from June, flower buds will begin to form. These are removed punctiliously until five to six weeks before a show, to prevent a premature flush of flower. (The exact timing of this is dictated by the cultivar, for some, like 'Roy Hartley' take longer to flower than the norm). About three weeks before the show, the two open female side flowers are removed to give the central male flower room to develop fully and to prevent fertilisation which would prematurely age the flower. From then on, she tries to keep the conditions as constant as possible, with good ventilation and only slight fluctuations in temperature and humidity. A week later, the bud will be 'oyster' shaped and from then on it is particularly important to maintain good ventilation.

Single-stemmed begonias for the 'boards'. Note Agnes Mowat's old net curtains, held up
with clothes-pegs, to shade the begonias from the sun. ·

Fortunately, Agnes' greenhouse has five large vents which can be opened. Just as the flowers are opening out, Agnes puts home-made cardboard collars around favoured flower heads: this prevents them from twisting and also keeps the leaves off the flowers. As each collar is nine inches wide, she knows she has a good flower if it grows to cover it. She was taught to do this by 'the old man', but has never seen it done by anyone else. She feeds her plants, once they are growing strongly, once a week with liquid 'Phostrogen' and a dose of Epsom salts if the leaves seem a little yellow, for Epsom salts contain magnesium. This feeding continues right up to show day.

There is no more delicate show flower than the begonia. The slightest touch on the stem with a watering can and it can rot and die off. Its cultivation is therefore fraught with particular difficulties as well as the more usual ones: how much and when to feed, what compost to use, and how to keep pests and diseases at bay. Mercifully, tuberous begonias are relatively immune to pest attack, except for the infamous red spider mite (the discouragement of which is one of the reasons why the relative humidity in the greenhouse must be kept high) and botrytis or grey mould, which flourishes in damp cold conditions in the autumn, particularly if dead leaves are not removed. Agnes lays much emphasis on cleanliness in the greenhouse, 'picking over' most days, and spraying with 'Benlate' at the first sign of fungal trouble.

Her greenhouse is a model of inventiveness. For example a wooden frame, on to which pea netting has been stretched, has been made to fit the doorway; in summer this is put in place to prevent the fledgling blackbirds from getting in, yet the begonias have the free circulation of air which they require. The greenhouse is painted with white shading and, on the inside, Agnes has hung her old net curtains to help prevent direct sunlight from getting in.

Peter has built special staggered wooden staging in the greenhouse on which to put the big clay pots. It is necessary because these pots are very heavy, yet must be easily accessible, for Agnes likes to turn them each day to encourage a good even head of flower, and also to pinch out the odd leaf if it is hiding a collection of new buds.

Like the other local exhibitors, Agnes tends to grow named varieties, usually obtained shortly after they first appear on the market by one grower and given as cuttings to some of the others. Popular show begonias are 'Mary Heatley' (soft orange), 'Sandra Lansley' (similar), 'Peach Melba' (primrose overlaid with orange), 'Roy Hartley' (pink), 'Bali-Hi' (cream with red picotee edge), 'Judy Langdon' (pale salmon-pink), and Agnes' great favourite, 'Tahiti' (an orange of startling vividness). None of the local showmen appears to do much breeding, although there are begonia breeders in south-west Scotland (notably in Sanquhar, thirty miles north of Dumfries), so that named and unnamed seedlings are sometimes distributed amongst the keen growers. 'Gay Gordon' is a successful show begonia which emanated from Sanquhar.

The fragility of begonias makes showing them a problem because they are so difficult to transport. Following the advice of 'the old man', Agnes places pieces of cotton wool between the flowers and the leaves in order to stop any bruising which might occur if they are rubbed together in transit. Like all exhibitors she also holds up the heavy flowers with special begonia head supports (the height of which can be easily adjusted); these have curved plastic tops ('stirrups') which gently hold the heads in place. Agnes will spend literally hours supporting every one of perhaps twenty flowers of a multi-stemmed plant in a large ten-inch-diameter pot, sometimes working late into the night by the light of an electric bulb on the eve of the show. It is absorbing work and must be done very carefully indeed. One shaky move and a precious 'head' will drop off. Begonias are one of the few show figures which can be put on the show bench with their supports visible, although good exhibitors do try to hide them behind the leaves if they can.

Agnes transports the big pots to the show in a milk crate while the single-stem begonias are already lodged in the 'boards'. 'The old man' also made a couple of begonia 'boards' for her, both of which she will need at Park Farm. Each is made of plywood, with four holes cut into it and covered with black material. Into each hole she puts a small plastic carton full of water to receive the cut head.

Accidents inevitably happen. Agnes was once taking a big 'Roy Hartley' to the show at Castle Douglas. It was almost the only one that she had left. 'I was that careful tying it up. A wee bit tighter with the string, a wee bit tighter, and the whole stem inside broke.' There was a big gap so she could not take it to the show. So she took the next best, and the man that won had one worse than hers. 'I maybe would have won!'

What Agnes enjoys most about showing is the staging of exhibits. This is not an elaborate process with begonias (most of it, in the way of supporting the begonias and scrubbing the pots, has been done at home already) but the begonias on the 'board' may need rearranging, labels need writing, and perhaps pots siting so that the weak flowers are less obvious to the judge.

Living right out in the country as she does, Agnes enjoys the opportunity of getting together with like-minded gardeners. There is great camaraderie between rivals at flower shows. However much it may be a matter of fierce pride to beat your opponent, you respect and often like him more than other acquaintances because he labours in the same vineyard. You may denigrate his prowess to others but you look forward to seeing him and discussing the finer points of cultivation, even if any questions have to be couched obliquely so as not to put him on his guard. For someone of Agnes' openness, who sees little point in keeping secrets and likes to encourage other exhibitors, staging is a marvellous opportunity for a 'blather'.

Over the last few years Agnes has won most of the cups for the begonias at the local shows, including the J. Kennlyside Silver Challenge Cup for the best plant at Park Farm in 1988. She likes the Park Farm show because it is the first one; she has obviously had enough by the last. 'It's grand when they're all finished. . . You're careful coming home from the show with your flowers in case you need them for the next one, but when you've gone to the last show you just shove everything

Agnes preparing 'Peach Melba' for show. She puts cotton wool to cushion every delicate flower from being rubbed by the leaves. The metal begonia head supports are just visible on the right side of the plant stems.

into the car, anyhow.' There is, I suspect, another reason why she likes the early shows: begonias usually start flowering in June and the biggest flowers tend to be on the early flushes; by the time of the late shows the flowers are getting progressively smaller. She is therefore in no hurry to start the tubers off in the spring, because the more the plants are disbudded to prevent them flowering, the higher (and therefore leggier and less satisfactory) will be the flowers when they *are* allowed to come.

Agnes shows other begonias as well, namely the so-called 'multiflora' or small-flowered type, such as the golden-yellow 'Flamboyant'. She also has two faithful cacti which regularly go as well, not to mention hybrid tea and floribunda roses. She usually puts in a 'board' of pansies and any amount of vases of cut border flowers, depending on what she has available. There are classes for vases of scabious, phlox, herbaceous (any other variety), antirrhinums, 'Scots' marigolds (*Calendula*), French marigolds, African marigolds, annuals, dahlias and gladioli. However, even in Scotland there was a drought and a hosepipe ban in 1989, so the week before the show she was uncertain what, apart from 'a few marigolds', she would be able to cut for the show. Curiously, she did not consider that the hot dry weather had affected her begonias too badly or encouraged them to flower much earlier than usual, probably because she had made strenuous efforts to bring the temperature down by ventilating the greenhouse and damping down the floor five times a day.

Agnes' willingness to help other exhibitors is particularly appreciated by Sandy Gordon, with whom she swaps cuttings and a variety of kindnesses. Sandy is in his early seventies and has been showing flowering pot plants, particularly gloxinias, since 1968 – ever since he recovered from an operation to amputate his right arm after an accident at work.

Sandy Gordon lives with his wife Martha in a neat council house in Shieldhill, a hamlet near Lochmaben, east of Dumfries. The house overlooks a small loch where the curlew calls. The Gordons have been married for more than fifty years and have lived in this house since it was first built some forty years ago. Sandy's father was a ploughman and his wife's father a hill shepherd.

At first sight it would seem impossible that a man with just one arm could grow pot plants so successfully that, like Agnes, he has won most of the cups to be had at local shows. Such success is the direct result of an uncommon determination to live a full life. The accident brought an end to his career as a long-distance lorry driver which had spanned thirty-five years. But over the next few years he taught himself to do a number of tasks with his left hand, including writing, driving an automatic car and digging the vegetable garden with a fork.

Sandy Gordon in the greenhouse where he grows begonias and gloxinias.

Sandy has always been a keen gardener, capable, despite being away for weeks on end, of maintaining a tidy and fruitful garden, and his retirement from driving gave him the opportunity to develop his taste for it. He began growing pot plants in earnest in two second-hand wooden greenhouses which he erected with the help of his son-in-law. (One cost £20, the other £100 – I never met a Dumfriesian exhibitor who had paid full price for one of these expensive structures.)

The year after his operation one of his daughters encouraged him to enter a gloxinia for the Castle Douglas show. A first prize gave him heart to continue. He is most interested in gloxinias (now strictly speaking called *Sinningia speciosa*), the deliciously-scented relatives of the begonia with velvety leaves and large trumpet flowers in sumptuous shades of pink, red, purple, blue, and white, and more often than not with the colour spotted on a white background.

It may be that one of the reasons he likes gloxinias is that they do not usually grow quite as big as the tuberous-rooted begonias and are therefore easier for him to handle. As he says, he cannot with one hand manage a pot bigger than eight inches in diameter (Agnes' multi-stemmed begonias are usually in ten-inch diameter pots) and he must use plastic pots whereas she prefers the heavier porous terracotta kind. There is little doubt that Sandy's misfortune has influenced what he grows. Pot plants appeal particularly because he feels he can manage them relatively easily, although in the past he has also shown vegetables, even 'pot' leeks which are generally acknowledged to be difficult to grow well. But he has given up growing incurved and semi-incurved chrysanthemums, because he could not grow them to his exacting standards. He found that he needed two hands to disbud them: using only one it was too easy to remove the terminal 'mother' bud by mistake. He will only show that which, with Martha's help, he can get to the show himself.

His disability has spurred him to an inventiveness which is impressive. As he says, he must think things out for himself. For example, in order to carry the pots in safety in the boot of his car, he has had made a set of heavy iron rings of varying diameters which neatly fit the circumference of the various pots. In his greenhouse he has erected a small propagating case, with soil-warming cables, for the gloxinias. The structure is made of wooden laths over which is stretched clear polythene, and the lid rests, when lifted, on a wooden ledge, so that the case can easily be opened with one hand. Most ingenious of all, however, is Sandy's answer to the adjustable begonia head support. The ordinary one requires two hands to adjust the height, but he has devised two different kinds: the first one has a cork at the end of the rod which, when pushed up, will stay in place; the second has flexible plastic instead of the cork which remains in the shape into which it has been squeezed.

Gloxinias are grown in much the same way as begonias: they require a winter dormant period and are then brought back into growth in boxes of moist peat in spring at a temperature of 16°–18°C (60–64°F). When the shoots are one or two inches high they are potted on individually into a free-draining peat compost, the tubers placed level with the surface. They like the same régime of high humidity, good shading, and a minimum temperature of 18° as suits the begonias, and must be kept well watered all season. They are fed every seven to ten days from the time the first flower bud appears, and are gradually dried off again as the winter approaches. Gloxinia tubers rarely last as long as begonia tubers, and so are propagated from leaf cuttings which are taken in early summer.

Growing a good show plant takes more skill than this suggests, particularly achieving a good display of flowers, rounded 'like a mushroom', which is the show ideal. Sandy's secret for achieving flowers of a uniform height is: 'When they're young plants . . . keep taking the inside leaves off them and let the heads [of flowers] out. . . I missed a cup at Kirkcudbright to a special gloxinia growing man and he said, "If you took your knife out of your pocket, and cut that one off, there's nothing in this hall to beat it."' One flower was about an inch above the rest in the middle of the plant; it needed to be taken off so that the flowers were level.

According to the entry in the 1981 RHS Handbook, the individual flowers should have 'a circular outline with rounded, overlapping lobes and the diameter of the tubes (throats) in proportion to the length of the lobes. Clear colours and distinct markings. Healthy foliage, of good substance, undamaged and clean.' Out of a maximum of twenty points, six can be given for the plant (vigour and flowering), five for the form of flower, five for the colour, and four for the foliage.

Sandy has some thirty-six gloxinias all together, and also grows pelargoniums, streptocarpus, achimenes, fuchsias, petunias in pots and approximately thirty begonias. Any two of these may go into the 'two-pot' class. Like other exhibitors Sandy feels the prestige of winning the 'two-pot' class, so the standard of entries, therefore, is always very high. As recognition of the difficulty inherent in growing two disparate pot plants well, the first prize is £4, the second £3 and the third £2, as opposed to £1 for first prize, seventy-five pence for second and fifty pence for third in the other classes.

Sandy's success has been considerable. In twenty years of showing at Kircudbright, for example, his gloxinias have only once been beaten. He is proudest of winning the special prize for the best pot plant at the Dumfries Octocentenary show in 1986, held at the Loreburn Hall in Dumfries (the show organized by the

Dumfries and District Horticultural Association on the August Bank Holiday weekend). 'I treasure that one more than any other.'

Some fifteen miles north-west of Dumfries stands the ancient house of Maxwelton, once the home of Annie Laurie, immortalized in William Douglas' poem. The gardens are the province of Willie Addison, a gamekeeper's son born in Peeblesshire, in his late thirties, whose round face and cheerful demeanour give him the look of a well-favoured monk. He is the model of what a single-handed head gardener should be: self-reliant, hard-working and resourceful, with an obvious and genuine love for what he does. And what he does is prodigious. He looks after gardens which extend to ten acres and include a productive kitchen garden and two large glasshouses.

Willie was trained 'in the old way' under the head gardener, Sandy Niven, at nearby Portrack, then home of Sir John Keswick. When he began to work there all he was allowed to do was wash pots and weed – for weeks on

LEFT Sandy's candidates for the prestigious 'two-pot' class, a streptocarpus and a gloxinia. Note the just visible plastic pot.

RIGHT One of the greenhouses under the care of Willie Addison at Maxwelton, showing the impressive range of pot plants that he grows.

end. Later, he graduated to cutting the grass – 'that was promotion'. (Small wonder that he disapproves of college-trained, 'training shoe' head gardeners). Finally, after thirteen years, he left to better himself and came to Maxwelton as gardener, at a time when the garden was becoming run down. The owner was thinking of pulling down the two handsome wooden greenhouses, but Willie's enthusiasm encouraged him to repair them. The garden is presently in fine fig and, the year after Willie's arrival in 1983, was opened to the public.

Willie's other great interest is taking his three dogs to beat and 'pick up' at local shoots, and he now looks after the pheasants on the Maxwelton estate as well. While still at Portrack he met Tommy Moffat, who was gamekeeper on Lord Perth's estate at Kinharvie, but was also a well-known local exhibitor of begonias and fuchsias. He gave Willie cuttings of both and persuaded his protégé in 1983 to join the flower show committee of the Dumfries and Lockerbie Agricultural Society. They have been friends ever since.

It was not until he came to Maxwelton that, with the blessing of his employer, Willie started entering plants into local shows. At the first one he went to, he showed a *Begonia rex* which took first prize, and he also won two 'seconds' and two 'thirds' – all with five plants. His ambition was fired but he reminisces ruefully about the elementary mistakes he made at first: 'Some of the stuff I was just lifting out of the greenhouse, taking it in and just putting it down, you know. I was not spending any time actually cleaning it off or presenting it properly'. He took dirty pots to the show until somebody said 'You might have washed your pots before you brought them in.'

Willie grows a wide variety of tuberous begonias in the warmer of the two greenhouses (mainly as single-stemmed plants so that he can cram more in) but these are purely for greenhouse display and he never shows them, except at those shows at Moniaive and Thornhill which are very close by. There is a simple reason for this: the road between Maxwelton and Dumfries is extremely windy, which means that he will inevitably lose some flower heads before he arrives at his destination. In any event, his great hobby is growing fuchsias, particularly the large standard fuchsias (those with a stem of more than thirty inches) and at that he is a master. The only problem, as he admits, is that he is a compulsive cuttings taker, so that instead of having three standard fuchsias (which is how many he has space for comfortably) he has thirty-six. Several of the local exhibitors have felt the benefit of Willie's success as a plant propagator.

Willie grows his fuchsias in the peach house, for they need only be kept frost free in winter. The 'standards', however, must be left to grow on ('green' is the gardener's word for it) in a minimum temperature of 10°C (50°F), and these overwinter in the warmer house.

They are grown in a John Innes compost, watered freely when they are growing and fed weekly with a liquid fertilizer. Much of the skill in growing them (apart from keeping the whitefly at bay) consists of pinching out all the laterals evenly either eight or ten weeks before the show (depending on whether it is a single or double-flowered variety) so that the shape will be round and uniform.

'Dressing' at the show, by removing the dead flowers and pulling out those which are hidden by leaves, is time-consuming but considered well worth the effort. To please the judges Willie tries to produce a symmetrical, floriferous plant, with clean foliage and fresh flowers of good colour. The head should be in proportion to the length of stem, in the case of a standard. Fuchsias are 'twenty point' flowers, of which a maximum of seven points are available for 'growth', seven points for the quantity and quality of the bloom, four for foliage and two for colour.

In 1989 Willie was rather pleased with two three-year-old standards of the almost hardy variety 'Charming'. It is single, has a deep red tube and sepals, and a red-purple corolla. A fuchsia to catch the judge's eye. One was to go into the 'two-pot' class, along with a very large specimen of a form of *Begonia rex*, and the other into the standard fuchsia class. He had a bush 'Mieke Meursing', a well-known show variety of proven worth with red sepals and pale pink corolla, to enter for the class of 'one fuchsia, bush, ball or shrub'.

Willie may baulk at transporting begonias, but a five-foot-tall fuchsia like the big 'Charming' is no picnic either. One year he took some large plants to the Dumfries Flower Show in the back of a borrowed cattle float, drawn by the family Fiesta. The plants were held upright by his brother Jimmy (who also shows pot plants with success at Dumfries), Willie's wife, and two children: 'Mind you, if the police had caught us it would have been the gaol'. Willie escaped with his liberty but the poor Fiesta needed new shock absorbers. In 1989 he decided that his brother's Land Rover would be a better bet to pull the cattle float. He made concrete blocks to fit round the pot bases to hold the plants steady in the trailer.

Of all the local showmen Willie is the most adventurous. This may have as much to do with his comparative youth as anything else. He is prepared to go as far as the Scottish Fuschia Society Show, held in mid-September at Linlithgow, and has won some prizes in classes competing against what he calls 'the big boys', the serious national exhibitors. The challenge appeals to him.

If there is any feeling locally that Willie has an advantage over his fellows because he is a professional gardener, it is more than tempered by a liking for the man himself. Although in the past there was perhaps some reason for the antagonism felt towards head

gardeners who took all the prizes at local shows at their employers' expense, in their employers' time, and often despite their employers' resentment, Willie has so much to do at Maxwelton and must make such a varied display for the visitors that he probably has no more time than amateurs to tend his plants. There is no distinction in the Park Farm schedule between amateurs and professionals, so plainly the committee does not see being a professional gardener as an advantage. Certainly, apart perhaps from the standard fuchsias, Willie does not grow anything specifically for show, but prefers to make a tour of the greenhouses the week before the show to see what might be suitable. He also shows peaches and other fruit from the garden. Winning prizes at shows is a clear indication of any person's skill as a cultivator and that pleases the professional just as much, if not more, as it does the amateur.

On the outskirts of Dumfries is the industrial suburb of Heath Hall. Here, in a bungalow, with about quarter of an acre of well-kept garden, lives Tom Blain, Chairman of the Dumfries and District Horticultural Association and a considerable and well-respected force in the district, both as enthusiastic exhibitor and show organizer. Hard-working and committed, he cares passionately about the whole business and, despite his job as supervisor of the traffic wardens in Dumfries and as a special constable, finds time to exhibit in six local shows

FAR LEFT Tom Blain chooses his begonias for the show in early August.

ABOVE Tom stages his begonias before going off to work. This one, destined for the 'board' needs a little attention.

during the summer, as well as judging at about three. He shows several kinds of vegetables, particularly potatoes, which he grows on an allotment in the town, but he reserves his best efforts for the large-flowered begonias.

Tom was brought up in Dunscore, a village between Dumfries and Moniaive, the son of a smallholder. Now in his fifties, he has gardened all his married life. He and his wife have lived in their present house for almost twenty years and have had a wooden greenhouse (bought second-hand, of course) for most of that time. One day in 1973 he met a friend of his, Sandy Niven, the head gardener from Portrack and Willie Addison's former boss, and, in the course of their conversation, Sandy Niven promised to supply his friend with some begonia tubers. On 5 May (he remembers the date because it is written on the labels of those which have survived) he received a baker's dozen of begonia tubers. 'I brought them home and I potted them up . . . and they looked well. Two or three days after that it was a warm day. The door was slightly open but I had no shading on it [the greenhouse]. When I came home at night they were all hanging limp. They'd been roasted. I didn't tell him. They came back but they didn't show any worthwhile blooms.' He had learned his lesson about shading.

Sandy Niven, a gardener of the old school, advised Tom to grow the begonias in clay, rather than plastic, pots, advice to which he has always adhered. He believes that the plant's root system develops better, because there is air exchange through the porous clay. He also uses a loam compost of his own devising, somewhere between John Innes 2 and 3, and waters in a half-strength feed of Phostrogen from six weeks before flowering. He now has an aluminium greenhouse as well to house his burgeoning collection, but prefers the wooden one because it stays cooler by up to 12 degrees Fahrenheit on hot days.

Tom first showed begonias in 1974, at Locharbriggs. Although the plant he showed was leggy, had no side shoots and the canes and supports were perfectly visible, so that it makes Tom blush to think of it, he won first prize. 'I got bitten with exhibiting and getting involved with horticultural shows. If you're prepared to work somebody will say, "Come on and join us".' However, it all really began in about 1970, when he had the Loreburn Hall on his beat one August Bank Holiday. In a quiet moment he wandered in and thought he should like to get involved because the atmosphere appealed to him.

He began by showing single-stemmed varieties and progressed to the big pots of multi-stemmed begonias. He believes that the begonia 'board' is the most difficult class to do well in, because the ideal has to be fresh, with a single centre, perfectly formed petals, a clear colour, circular and of a uniform size. To get four that fit those criteria, and especially that match each other in size, is very hard indeed. Roses and begonias are not the only

flowers, incidentally, which are put on 'boards' to show off their individual beauty: pansies and violas are displayed in this way as well.

Tom has won cups at most of the local shows in his time, and even ventured as far as Ayr Show. The Scottish Begonia Society have their annual competition at Ayr and there are classes for the various colours of begonias and even a 'board' for twelve begonia heads. It was a trip to Ayr in 1977 which decided Tom against using pieces of cotton wool between petals and leaves. He remembers that there was hail and snow even though it was almost the end of August. It was two o'clock in the morning when they carried the pots into the hall and everything got soaking wet. He found that trying to pull the bits of fluff out was not at all easy. He depends now solely on the begonia supports.

The size of the begonias in the pots is a source of surprise, even irritation, to other show visitors. 'There was one old boy at . . . and he was rather annoyed because I had big pots.' He queried whether Tom had two tubers in the pot. 'Anyway this old character thought that he would try and have a look and he was really going in to spoil the plant. And I told him quite clearly that he had no right to touch it. . . He didn't take it politely.' The problem is that a begonia tuber is immensely susceptible to rot if damaged, even slightly, by a pencil or knife blade, and no devoted begonia grower can view damage to a ten-year-old tuber with equanimity.

As chairman of a horticultural society, Tom has certain ideas about those who show. He believes, for example, contrary to the popular orthodoxy, that prize money is important to many exhibitors: 'It's money that fills the petrol tank; its money that fills the greenhouse.' He believes that many showmen disguise the fact that they are attracted by cash prizes. Certainly at the show held in the Loreburn Hall, which is organized by his association, the prize for the best exhibit in the Blue Riband class is £25 and there is no shortage of entries.

In 1989, Tom found the hot summer rather trying for his begonias. They flowered in a shorter space of time than the usual six to eight weeks, which put out his timing for the various shows. He had also lost his prize-winning 'Bali-Hi' the year before. As a full-time traffic warden he could only water in the early morning and evening when he came home from work, which meant that he could not damp down the floors of the greenhouse five times a day as Agnes was able to do in the hottest weather in July. So the flowers of some suffered from colour blotching as a result of the excessively high temperatures. Nevertheless, he was philosophical and hoped to have a good pot of 'Peach Melba' to go into the 'two-pot' class with a faithful *Begonia rex*. Like Agnes, he was hoping to find pots to show which were well-balanced plants, bearing a good many large flowers, of

good substance, circular in outline with broad overlapping petals culminating in one centre (as opposed to a divided centre). The colour should be decided and clear and the foliage clean, healthy and undamaged. Out of a maximum of twenty points, the plant could receive five, the stems three, the form of flower six, the colour three, and the foliage three.

The Convenor of the flower show section at Park Farm is Tommy Moffat, a man held in great esteem by the Dumfries exhibitors. He has been a successful begonia and fuchsia grower in the past but, although only in his

ABOVE LEFT The Convener of the 'Flowers, Vegetables, Fruit and Floral Art' section, Tommy Moffat, answers a query from Agnes during staging.

ABOVE RIGHT Tom and Agnes' begonia 'boards'. Tom's, on the left, consists of 'Gay Gordon' and 'Jean Ishbell' on the top, 'Alice Talbot' and 'Alec Grierson' on the bottom. Agnes', on the right, has 'Robert Spence' and 'Gay Gordon' above, with two 'Judy Langdon' below.

late sixties, his uncertain health now restricts him to organization rather than exhibition. He is a retired gamekeeper.

The work of Tommy and his committee, which comprises some young men like Willie Addison and his brother Jimmy (a foreman in the Dumfries Parks

ABOVE LEFT Judging the pot plant classes. Sandy's white petunia can clearly be seen at the back, as can one of Willie Addison's standard fuchsias, 'Charming'. In the front are Sandy's two prize-winning gloxinias.

ABOVE RIGHT A triumphant Willie with the winners of the 'two-pot' class, *Fuchsia* 'Charming' and a form of *Begonia rex*. The begonia also won him the cup for the best pot-plant in the show.

Department), consists of drawing up, having printed, and sending out the schedules, inviting the judges, and arranging the staffing on the day.

Show schedules are sent out early, in April, to give potential exhibitors plenty of time to see what is required of them and to plan accordingly. In the main, a committee will have considerable natural reluctance about altering a schedule unless, as Tommy Moffat says, a class is 'not working', that is the numbers of entries are declining markedly. On the whole, however, committees keep to the time-hallowed classes in deference to the conservatism of the exhibitors. I mean that word in no derogatory sense, for it is inevitable that people will assume that there are no alterations year on year. The most changes are to be found in the children's section (for children enjoy novelty) and in the floral art (called in Dumfries the 'decorative classes') because it is not appropriate to ask flower arrangers to work to the same theme two years in succession. One of the themes in 1989, for example, was 'The Farming Centenary', a subject which would not bear repeating.

The entries must be in by Tuesday night so that the committee knows how many there are to be and can write out entry cards. He goes in on Wednesday evening (before the Friday of showday) with most of his male colleagues and sets up all the staging for the exhibitors coming in on Thursday night to stage. Even if a committee is strict about not allowing late entries (and not all show committees are), it is a taxing task allocating the right length of staging so that there is enough, but not too much, space for each exhibit. 'The lady members [of the committee] normally come in on Thursday morning and they set up their section for the floral art. But I'm in charge of the whole set-up so I have got to be there really all the time, from the Wednesday night until we finish up on the Sunday morning clearing the staging'. He sees the judges get a cup of coffee before the judging begins at eleven o'clock on Friday and lunch afterwards as well. 'It's a wee bit tiring . . . but I enjoy it.'

Members of the committee are allocated as stewards to help the judges, to write down the results, and deliver them to Tommy at the central table. He and his helpers must enter them in a ledger and write out prize cards, finishing the task before the show opens to the public.

Unlike many shows, here there is no points cup, only cups for the best exhibit in each section: pot plants; decorative section; cut flowers; vegetables; junior floral art; and children's horticultural classes. The judges decide the cup winners last of all. It is rarely an easy decision because they are not judging like with like.

In recent years the entries at Park Farm have kept up well and the standard is excellent, according to Tommy Moffat, who should know. He thinks that the prize money may attract some, although he agrees with Agnes that you usually finish out of pocket at these shows, however successful you are. This committee, like all others, has complaints to deal with from time to time, from competitors who have presumably failed to read the noble sentiments expressed in the RHS Handbook. Tommy's attitude towards any complaint is robust: 'I just say the committee's decision is final and it's left at that. We just stick [by the judge's decision]. That's it . . . we don't bother . . .' He has nothing but admiration for his committee. 'We've got a very hard-working committee . . . you just say the word and they're there.' Having seen the show I have no reason to disbelieve him, but there will be flower show committee members reading this who may well sigh with envy.

In 1989, as usual, the competitors staged their exhibits on Thursday evening and Friday morning, judging began at eleven o'clock, and the 'Pavilion' was open to visitors from three o'clock and for the whole of the next day. Tommy was pleased with both the quality and quantity of entries, despite the exigencies of the unusual season. Tom staged his begonias early, before going off to work. Agnes had to take care with the begonias to see that she removed every piece of cotton wool from them. She put two entries in the 'any begonia (large flowered type)' class, but Tom saved his efforts for the 'two-pot' class and the begonia 'boards'. Despite the many classes that she entered, Agnes still found time for a 'blather' with Sandy. Sandy entered several pot classes, including the 'two-pot' class with a gloxinia and a streptocarpus, the geranium (pelargonium) class, the 'foliage plant' class and the 'any other flowering plant' class which gave him an opportunity to show a thirty-six-inch tall single white petunia, (he likes to use a white petunia for this because the colour is set off well against the foliage). Sandy had high hopes of winning the best pot plant cup for this petunia, taking it away from the begonias which usually win it. Willie confined his efforts to the fuchsia and succulent classes, and the 'two-pot' class.

Agnes had first and second in the large-flowered begonia class, first in the small-flowered begonia class with 'Flamboyant', second with an achimenes in the 'any other flowering plant', and first and second in the cacti class, with two cacti which regularly win for her at shows during the summer. Both her begonia 'boards' had first prize, so Tom Blain had to be content with second place. Sandy's white petunia won the flowering plant class, his gloxinias were first and second in the gloxinia class, an iresine came second in the foliage plant class, and his succulent was also second. However, he had no luck in the 'two-pot class' as his plants were competing with those in rather bigger pots. Willie won both individual fuchsia classes with 'Mieke Meursing' and his standard 'Charming' respectively, first for a succulent plant and foliage plant, and he beat the luckless Tom Blain into second place in the 'two-pot' class. Tom could console himself that he had just failed in an excellent class. It was really Willie's day because his *Begonia rex*, which paired 'Charming' in the 'two-pot' class, was judged best in the section and won him the J. Kennlyside Cup. Sandy, who had such hopes for his petunia, was disgusted with himself: in the flurry of activity he forgot to remove the string which he had used to keep the flower heads together while he transported them to the show. The judge told him afterwards that, but for that, his petunia would have taken the cup for the best pot plant. 'I've only myself to blame' was his rueful comment.

CHAPTER THREE

ABERYSTWYTH

Aberystwyth and District Agricultural Society's
Annual Show

The coastline of Cardigan Bay curves as if it were all that remained after a giant had taken a mouthful of west Wales. More than halfway down the bay stands the town of Aberystwyth. The self-confident university buildings, the rack-and-pin railway, the Camera Obscura and the Marine Terrace proclaim Aberystwyth as a cosmopolitan town, but it is also the business and trading centre for the surrounding countryside, hosting a livestock market every other Monday.

The town lies on a narrow coastal strip which soon gives way to the east to rising hills dissected by rivers, two of which, the Ystwyth and Rheidol, flow into the sea at Aberystwyth. The hinterland is rural, and predominantly Welsh-speaking, although the inhabitants admit that their Welsh is not as pure as that spoken further north in Gwynedd, because they pepper their conversation with English words.

Each year, on the second Saturday in June, an agricultural show is held just outside Aberystwyth. It is said to be the largest one-day show in Wales. It is particularly noted for the quality of the Welsh cob ponies but, like most agricultural shows, it also has a produce tent. Because the show takes place far too early in the season for the classic show exhibits, like onions, dahlias, and chrysanthemums, the showmen concentrate on a mixture of early produce – lettuces, rhubarb, gooseberries, radishes and summer garden flowers – those which have no particular season, such as pot plants, notably cacti and succulents, and flower arranging, known to its devotees as 'floral art'.

Floral art is one of the most flourishing sections of the average produce tent. Much of the credit for this must go to NAFAS, the acronym for the National Association of Flower Arrangement Societies, which was founded in 1959 as the umbrella organization for the many local floral clubs which were springing up all over the country. Until then, the rules governing competitive flower arrangement were devised and regulated by a committee

of the RHS; that organization thankfully relinquished the burden when NAFAS was founded and the floral art classes at shows are now usually judged by NAFAS rules. There are presently about 1200 local clubs, many further education classes, and 120,000 members of NAFAS – which is comparable with what the Royal Horticultural Society itself can boast. The traditionalist may question the place of floral art in a flower show for it is not the quality of the produce which is under scrutiny but rather the artistic interpretation of the plant material; in the same way, some do not consider that 'ice dancing' is a proper Olympic sport. Whatever the rights or wrongs, floral art has undoubtedly brought many people, particularly women, into showing who would not otherwise compete.

Most flower arrangers become show competitors after joining a local flower club (where they will see demonstrations by a member of a national network of demonstrators provided by NAFAS) or after attending adult education classes. There is a measure of agreement as to what factors make a good exhibit, but they are not always apparent to the layman just by looking at the work of others. Show flower arranging appears to be most easily, or certainly congenially, learned in a class, rather than at home with books – which is the way many other horticultural exhibitors learn their craft. But then the importance of the social aspect of flower arranging should never be underestimated.

One of the most successful local exhibitors in the floral art classes is Mary Ellis. She and her husband Herbert, a retired painter and decorator, live in a square-fronted stone house in Talybont, about seven miles north of Aberystwyth. Mary is energetic, excitable, kindly, and immensely talkative. Herbert is a mild-mannered man who is good-naturedly tolerant of his wife's enthusiasms.

The Ellises have lived in the same house since 1960. It is surrounded on all sides by a well-kept and favoured garden of roses, vegetables and perennials, and contains two greenhouses (including one for peaches and grapes) and a little orchard. It is fruitful and gay in summer with half-hardy annuals. On the lawn in front of the house is a monkey-puzzle tree, under which Mary grows many shrubs and plants, including echinops, poppies, wormwood, paeonies, hellebores and acanthus, all of which come in very useful 'for the floral art', not to mention cacti, which spend their summer disposed around a painted hand plough.

In about 1970 Mary joined the newly-formed floral art club in Aberystwyth and began attending flower arrangement classes. Floral art demonstrators who came to Aberystwyth Flower Club saw her potential and she was encouraged by one of them, in about 1974, to enter the classes at the Royal Welsh Show in Builth Wells. So one evening after work she took a dried arrangement entitled 'A Winter's Tale' (her memory for the titles and plant material used in long-gone flower arrangements is prodigious) the hour's drive to Builth and achieved a Highly Commended in a class with thirty entries. In 1981 the theme was 'Our Heritage': her scheme consisted of a Welsh harp constructed out of a piece of polished 'driftwood', with bulrush stems as 'strings', together with a Welsh hat and shawl. In the hat she placed pink Brompton stocks and euphorbias surrounded by hosta leaves. For this she was awarded the Breconshire Cup.

In 1984 the paint and wallpaper shop in Talybont which Mary ran as part of her husband's business was sold. She then had more spare time, although she maintains that she was doing just as well when she had none. That said, it is obviously helpful to her not to have to go out to work any more because flower arrangers, if they want to enter several classes in a show, must work harder than any other horticultural exhibitor. It can be very exhausting, particularly at a show such as Aberystwyth, where Mary is eligible to enter seven classes.

She has an excellent sense of colour and composition, something often noted by the examiners who, unlike horticultural judges, make a point of commenting on the good and bad aspects of an exhibit – sometimes to the consternation of the exhibitor, for floral art judges can be very stern. She is also well known for the care she takes in drying her materials, and the skill with which she grows her plants. The system of working to themes, known as

interpretation, which seems to apply universally, suits her very well: 'I don't seem to be able to do [just] a vase of flowers nowadays.'

'Driftwood' figures very prominently in her (and many other arrangers') exhibits. It is not strictly speaking driftwood, as it is rarely washed up on the seashore; far more often it consists of pieces of tree root found on Sunday walks in the woods and cleaned up, polished and preserved by Herbert. It is apparently important that these pieces of wood should not be stained or highly varnished. The exhibitor must be very careful not to put driftwood in any class which specifically requires live plant material; Mary once missed a first prize at a show by making that mistake.

She uses a very wide range of plants in her arrangements, including a purple-leaved succulent aeonium from Madeira, much admired by members of the Flower Club. Large-flowered alliums, pink thalictrum and hosta leaves appear regularly in her June arrangements. She also has a rich fund of 'accessories', including a large, wide-bellied glass bottle half-filled with marbles.

She likes to sort out her accessories, and cut and gather her plant material, on Thursday for the Saturday show, so that she can spend Friday arranging the two miniature exhibits (which she is allowed to arrange at home) and practising the others. She never sketches out her designs but carries all ideas in her head. She does

Mary Ellis in her garden in Talybont picking pink thalictrum for an arrangement, on the Thursday before showday in early June.

admit to thinking about it a great deal. She is not influenced by others: 'Nobody tells me how to do it . . . I must have it my way.'

In 1989 the classes were grouped under the general theme of 'Flowers, food and farming'. There were eight classes in all, but one was for novices – those who have never won a first prize before. They were to be judged under NAFAS rules. The schedule allowed for only one entry per competitor, for these arrangements take up far more room than three carrots, say, or a collection of herbs. In 1989, the rules had been changed and all the entries, except the 'miniature' and 'petite', had to be assembled in the tent rather than at home. This was probably sensible because of the considerable difficulties involved in transporting a thirty-inch driftwood and hosta leaf ensemble, and perhaps it was even fairer, but it was bound to be a trial to all those who find working to a deadline paralysing. For Mary, it was a great anxiety.

Mary tries very hard to grow most of her flowers and foliage in the garden to keep the cost of flower arranging to manageable proportions. Her hostas, for example, are grown in tubs outside the back door, where they are out of harm's, or certainly slugs', way. Occasionally she will buy a few carnations or gerberas, but she is much less dependent on what is available in florists' shops than many amateur arrangers. Generally speaking the prizes for winners in the floral art section are rather more generous than is the case with other produce, reflecting the additional costs involved. At Aberystwyth, for example, the first prize is £3, as opposed to £2 in the horticultural section. But the entry fee is higher at twenty-five pence instead of fifteen, and the smallest lump of essential 'oasis' costs at least twenty pence.

In 1989 Mary showed at Talybont, Llangethor, Taliesin and Capel Bangor. These days she does not venture too far afield (apart from the Royal Welsh Show) because the work is so time-consuming, preferring instead to enter many classes in the local shows. Apart from the floral art she shows fruit, garden flowers, roses, geraniums, and cacti and succulents.

Fortunately her other main exhibits for Aberystwyth Show – cacti and succulents – take rather less energy to prepare for the show. They need little packing, except for placing in boxes with a great quantity of newspaper. The large specimens naturally disqualify themselves for showing, in any event, because they are too heavy in their terracotta pots to be carried.

Her passion for cacti and succulents started when she was given an echinocactus ('Golden Barrel') by an aunt. One day, as Herbert tried to open a sticking window above the cactus, his hand slipped and became impaled. It swelled immediately and turned a livid red. So vexed was Mary that, rightly or wrongly, she plunged Herbert's hand in hot water, and then threw the cactus away. The

Mary and Herbert in the cactus greenhouse with a flowering echinopsis.

next day his hand was so much better that she went back to the rubbish bin, fished out the offending cactus and reinstated it.

At some point the schedule makers at Talybont Show instituted a class for cacti, which encouraged Mary to continue to grow them, and she now has a substantial collection, mainly *Cleistocactus*, *Cephalocereus*, *Opuntia*, *Echinocactus* and *Cereus*, and succulents like *Kalanchoë*, *Crassula* and *Echeveria*. She does not know all their names, having acquired them mainly as presents from garden-minded neighbours. Her collection is housed in the white-painted wooden lean-to greenhouse on the side of the house; it is unheated but faces south-west.

To those who have never grown them (and there are plenty of very keen gardeners who can honestly say they never have), cacti may seem unattractive and stolid, sitting neglected on sunny windowsills where they hardly, if ever, flower. Perhaps they are thought too easily cultivated to warrant attention but, in fact, to grow them well, particularly well enough to show, is not at all easy. And a large, healthy cactus in full flower is a stunning sight.

Like most cactus growers, Mary does not water her plants between September and March. She grows them in a compost of her own devising, which seems principally to consist of molehill soil ('he [the mole] has been very kind to me'), peat and compost. She feeds them with cactus fertilizer regularly. She propagates a cactus by cutting off the top, leaving it for two or three days, plunging the end into flowers of sulphur, and then placing it on top of a pot filled with gritty compost. Her methods, whether intuitive or book-learned, seem to work well. She maintains that she just likes to grow things, and she likes to give them away.

Mary is an instinctive gardener, tending to read about plants after she has cultivated them rather than before, and often finding that she is already doing what is suggested. She seems to have a natural affinity with plants, and the all-important capacity for taking pains which is a common feature amongst successful showmen. She also talks openly to her plants, a habit which provides her with a ready source of material for her brand of disarming self-mockery.

For Mary, preparation for the show means giving the large cacti a thorough brush with one of Herbert's old paint brushes, for they do seem to attract the dust (she also has to do this when they return from the show, for canvas tents are even dustier than greenhouses). She then brushes them with a home-made soap, a mixture of fat, caustic soda and water. This is then rinsed off in clean water.

The 1981 RHS Handbook has this to say about what constitutes a meritorious cactus or succulent: '*A large specimen for the species* [which requires the judge to know the species], *well-balanced, in good health* [that is, no telltale woolly patches hiding mealy bug], *free from injury of any sort including damaged spines or defective "bloom"* [not the flower but the "bloom" on the leaves and stems of succulents such as echeverias, similar to the "bloom" on plums or grapes]. *Other things being equal, a plant which is in flower will be preferred to one which is not. A species or form which is rare in cultivation will be preferred to one which is common* [this also requires above average knowledge on the part of the judge].'

Points are awarded out of twenty, as follows: eight for condition, four for difficulty of cultivation, four for conformity of type and four for rarity. The second and fourth criteria are not usually the subjects for points in the judging of flowers: the usual ones are condition, form, colour, size and uniformity.

Mary transports the cacti to the shows in their clay pots wedged with newspaper in an old preserving pan. 'I find the small ones get the prizes now, so it isn't worth it going to kill yourself.' In 1989 she chose to take a flowering mammillaria and a very fine, yellow-flowering *Echinopsis aurea* (syn. *Lobivia aurea*) for the cactus class, not to mention the green *Opuntia cylindricata* 'Cristata' which won her first prize the year before for the succulent class, although strictly speaking, it is a cactus as well as a succulent.

Herbert helps her carry the pots to the show ground, together with all the materials for flower arranging. Mary depends on him for assistance and, even more, to enter the tent after the judging has finished and come out to tell her how she has done, while she sits nervous and exhausted in the car. She says she can always tell by the look on his face.

With a frankness which is by no means universal amongst competitors, Mary admits that it is the excitement of winning which spurs her on: 'I do like to come home with one prize.' She usually comes home with rather more than that, having won the Perpetual Challenge Silver Rose Bowl for the most points in the floral art section at Aberystwyth Show in 1988.

John Ockey's approach is rather more consciously scientific. He is an outgoing and amusing retired vet who lives with his wife Margaret in Llanbadarn, on the outskirts of Aberystwyth. He has a south-facing conservatory filled with dozens of different species of cacti and succulents, none of which he has any difficulty in naming.

He probably would not grow them, were it not for a love of botany he acquired during his time as a student of veterinary medicine at the University of Liverpool during the war. He thinks that is why he is so keen on *Cactaceae*, an enormous and immensely complicated family, some of whose members differ only minutely from each other. To

a man who learned to identify grasses by pulling them apart and staring at them through a hand-lens, the counting of spines or hairs seems perfectly natural. A fondness for plant taxonomy, and a liking for Latin names, is extremely helpful for those growing a large collection of cacti.

He spent his childhood in the East End of London where his father was a policeman, but his family were farmers in Herefordshire and childhood holidays were spent there. After graduating as a vet he began in private practice, but after a while he joined the Ministry of Agriculture in the West Midlands for a trial period – 'and stayed thirty years'. He enjoyed Ministry work because it meant a great deal of diagnostic work and he liked dealing with national problems.

Like Mary Ellis, John Ockey has a refreshing line in self-mockery. He appreciates that there are many who think that cactus growers are quite simply mad. He says that most people think that cacti are dull, tatty things which never flower. He is right: the very amenability of many commonly available cacti means they are disregarded and ignored. John grows as many different kinds as he can because he likes to see the range. What he really enjoys is seeing cacti and succulents in their native

John Ockey combs the cephalium of the 'Old Man' cactus, *Cephalocereus senilis*, which he will put in the cactus class. Behind are some of his cactus collection, notably espostoas and cereuses.

surroundings, something he has managed to do in Utah and Nevada.

The first cacti John grew were 'Woolworth's throw-outs' bought in 1958 or 1959. But until the Ockeys erected a small six-foot by four-foot greenhouse, when they were living in Shrewsbury in the early 1960s, his interest extended only as far as cultivating a few cacti on a windowsill. The acquisition of a greenhouse was precipitated by a most unfortunate incident. Their cleaning lady, a woman of ample proportions, was leaning over the cacti (which now filled every inch of windowsill) one day to clean the windows and was impaled on a barbed spine belonging to an opuntia (prickly pear), which became wedged in her cleavage. Rather than lose her, the Ockeys banished the cacti to a greenhouse, and John had the opportunity to expand his collection.

In 1965 he received some seed from his brother, who was studying as an agricultural botanist in Houston, Texas. This partly explains why, for an amateur, he grows such a large number of species, many of them uncommon. Some of the plants from that seed still live in the greenhouse for, if looked after, cacti will survive a long time. Fortuitously, at the same time John lived near enough to Bridgnorth to visit the famous cactus garden belonging to General Oliver Leese, and learned a great deal from wandering around the garden in his lunch hours.

Not everyone who grows cacti wishes to show them, by any manner of means; indeed, many with a scientific bent shrink from the idea. However, John had joined the Gloucester Cactus Club when he and his wife went to live in Hereford in 1965, and the club encouraged its members to show. It held its own monthly shows, often concentrating on a specific genus, say *Mammillaria* or *Cereus*, and he learned how to present his material to the best advantage by listening to the experiences of other club members. The club also exhibited at the specialist cactus shows held at Stroud and Cheltenham. John had some notable successes, about which he is modest: for example, a bronze medal for the best pair of mammillarias shown at Cheltenham in 1970.

That year the Ockeys moved to Haverfordwest in west Wales but, although John continued to exhibit, the general standard was much lower than that of shows he had been used to attending. In 1980 he came to Aberystwyth to work and retired from the Ministry in 1986. In 1988 he showed at Aberystwyth Show, the first time he had exhibited for eight years, winning a third for his 'Golden Barrel', *Echinocactus grusonii*.

Taxonomically the family *Cactaceae* is fascinating. All cacti are succulents but not all succulents are cacti. It is as well to know the difference if you are showing them, for in many shows there are separate classes for each. The simplest definition of a cactus is that it has 'areoles'. These look like tiny pincushions and are the sites from

which the spines and flowers emerge. Other succulents, such as *Hoya*, *Aloe*, *Kalanchoë* and *Crassula*, do not have them. Cacti do everything – transpire, flower and root – at the areoles. Botanists regard the areole, and the conformation of the spines, as very important diagnostic features, because they differ from species to species.

Cultivation of cacti is not usually tricky, but there are some species which cause difficulties by rotting off easily such as the yellow-spined parodias. Amongst the easiest are *Mammillaria* (although not *M. bombycina* or *M. plumosa*), *Rebutia*, *Aylostera*, *Echinocereus* and *Lithops*. Few are genuinely hardy, and they need to be grown in some shelter; but the average small amateur greenhouse is not ideal, because it gets too hot in summer and too cold in winter. Attention must therefore be paid to ventilation and shading, and a war must be waged against mealy bug and red spider mite. On the whole cacti and succulents are not difficult to keep alive, but to grow a good show specimen, without marks and with equidistant spines, takes consistent cultivation.

John uses an open, well-drained soil-based compost for potting. He avoids peat-based composts, such as are now so common for most kinds of pot plants, because, as he points out, the vast majority of cacti are lime-loving. The mixture is usually one third John Innes No 1 or 2, one third grit and one third perlite. He finds perlite much better than vermiculite because the latter degenerates into a 'sludgy mess', whereas perlite retains its shape almost indefinitely. As he says, many cacti are mountain plants, capable of growing well above 3,000 feet in full sun and with perfect drainage, so he is inclined to treat them as alpines, even to the extent of putting half an inch of coarse grit on top of the compost to help prevent basal rot.

Because they are perennials, and often slow-growing, cacti do not need potting every year, indeed they are more likely to flower if left in a small pot (in this respect they are similar to many other plants, which will flower when put under stress). On the other hand, if a cactus is in too large a pot for its roots, it may well rot.

John's visit to the western states of America convinced him that, contrary to popular belief, deserts are not all sand; they are also made up of rock and some good soil, which is rich in potash. Bearing this in mind, he feeds his cacti every fortnight in the summer with a high potash feed. They are watered about once a week, except in hot weather in high summer when the watering may have to be rather more frequent.

John confesses to being rather lazy about his cacti and succulents these days. Perhaps it is the lack of the spur of fierce competition, for he says he would be showing more seriously if he still lived in the West Midlands. Fortunately these plants lend themselves to part-time gardening, for they can be left for almost half the year without any attention at all. All the plants in the conservatory on the side of the house are covered in plastic sheeting from the end of October until late March to protect the plants from the worst of the winter, and are hardly watered at all, except for 'a monthly trickle' given to the South African epiphytes and the succulents. Because the conservatory is barely heated at all, in bad weather there can be adverse effects on a few of the tall, columnar cereuses and epiphyllums, which do require slightly higher temperatures than the others in winter. They show their disapproval by developing marks. However, this relaxed approach does leave John and his wife free to help with the lambing on their son-in-law's farm in the Black Mountains.

In March John gives all the cacti and succulents a soaking with soft water, which, as he says, shakes them up and causes the round pads of opuntias to fall off. These pads very often root on top of the soil in the pot, no doubt responding as they would to the short-lived desert rains. In theory, at least, he waters the plants from the base of the pots, not overhead. Any splashes of water on the stems can cause a mark if the sun is strong enough to act as a magnifying glass.

For many people, myself included, the growing of cacti is made impossible by a morbid fear of the spines. John tends to discount such fears, quite rightly pointing out that not all cacti are spined and, of those that are, only the ones with hooked or barbed spines (like opuntias) are dangerous. That said, his hands do bear the scars of old wounds, and he suspects that one or two spines may even have damaged tendons in his hands – and that despite carefully wrapping the cacti in newspaper when he handles them or wearing extremely thick gloves. He also finds a pair of artery forceps (not normally an item in the gardener's toolshed) very useful for the delicate operation of removing seedheads, or for dabbing cotton wool soaked in methylated spirits amongst the spines to kill the mealy bug, one of the worst enemies of cacti.

He propagates his plants in the same way as Mary does, by simply placing the cut surface of one on top of the sand after it has been allowed to dry out somewhat. If buried, they rot. He even knows how to graft them. This he does by taking a common kind with a good rootstock, such as an opuntia or a pereskia, and joining it with a long spine to a cut scion, selected because it does not usually make strong roots, such as one of the hanging epiphyllums.

John no longer shows his cacti seriously, in his terms, but is content to keep his hand in at Aberystwyth. He has some misgivings about the standard of the judging at local shows, which arises out of the knowledge that not all general flower judges know very much about cacti and succulents, or certainly not all the many kinds which enthusiasts like John grow.

John says that in a specialist show the exhibitor has to make sure that his plant is what he says it is. Specialist judges know because they are trained. The pot must be clean and have the right soil covering, which is half an inch of grit. The plant must be the right size for the pot, which means repotting it when the spines reach the edge. The size of the plant does not necessarily matter, but rather how it has been grown, how healthy it looks and, particularly, the coloration and even spacing of the spines. Flowers are not necessarily important; for example *Echinocactus*, the 'Golden Barrel', will not flower until it has reached a size too large and heavy to be got to the show. Aylosteras and rebutias, on the other hand, flower regularly but they may not flower at the same time as the show.

After deciding to enter a show, the first thing that John does is to get hold of the schedule to see what is required in the classes. In the case of the Aberystwyth Show he is allowed two entries per class, which means two cacti and two succulents. Then he looks to see what he has that is looking well. The day before, he will clean up the show specimens, washing them carefully in fine detergent, and even going to the lengths of combing the cephalia (woolly caps which form at the top of some cacti, for instance *Espostoa* or *Cephalocereus senilis*, the 'Old Man' cactus), first with an old toothbrush and then with a comb. To do this he has to put on his strongest gloves and, holding the pot away from him, comb the hairs the way that they grow, which is usually in concentric rings.

The next day, he wraps the plants in newspaper so that the spines of one will not damage another and the pots are put in boxes which are also padded with newspaper: 'You then have to drive at about two miles an hour all the way.' One of the greatest problems is the flowers: many of them last for only about twenty-four hours and they drop off with appalling ease.

John believes that an old specimen can be successful at a show, particularly if it is clean and has no marks on it. Marking and ridging on the stems is usually a result of drought at some point in a growing season, and never disappears; this is because the cactus does not die down to ground level each year like most other non-woody perennials. It is therefore very difficult to grow a cactus for a long period of time without these disfiguring marks and ridges appearing.

Size and colour have an effect, too. He remembers winning first prize for aloes (succulents) at Gloucester one year, because he had the Partridge-Breasted Aloe (*Aloe variegata*) in a twelve-inch pan. It was beautifully coloured and the sun had brought out the striations. 'What you *don't* want is a green, juicy thing which is

RIGHT Dan and Eirlys Davies, having collected some of the produce which will be going to the show.

totally against what they're like in nature.' Mary might disagree for her green opuntia, which had been kept in a dark shed, won in 1988 at Aberystwyth. This illustrates neatly the gap that exists between generalists and specialists in showing, a gap which partly explains why specialist growers are not always to be found supporting their local show.

In 1989, John took to Aberystwyth Show a rare and well-grown *Mammillaria bombycina* and a more common *Cephalocereus senilis* for the cactus class, *Echeveria setosa* 'Doris Taylor', which has a long bending spike of yellow-tipped red flowers, and *Euphorbia obesa*, a globose succulent spurge with pronounced ribs, for the succulent class.

Dan Davies is the classic generalist. He enters as many classes as anyone in the Produce Tent at the Aberystwyth Show and, in 1988, for the third year running, came away with the Silver Cup for the highest number of points. If he has a preference it is for flowers, particularly sweet peas and dahlias, but he is prepared to enter anything that he has available and in good condition, from apples to delphiniums. People such as Dan Davies warm the hearts of show organizers for they swell the numbers of entries with good quality produce.

Dan and his wife Eirlys live in the strikingly beautiful Rheidol valley, about halfway between Aberystwyth and

Devil's Bridge. Their small whitewashed farmhouse stands in the lee of a hill covered by Forestry Commission conifers. Clearly to be seen clinging to the edge of the hill on the other side of the valley is the steam train which puffs its way from Aberystwyth to Devil's Bridge each day in the summer. The half-acre garden in front and to the side of the house faces south. It would be very favoured were it not for the cold east winds and late frosts, the very heavy and stony soil, and the destructive squirrels and magpies which shelter in the woodland behind.

Eirlys has always lived here, for the house belonged to her grandparents who looked after their daughter and granddaughter while her father worked in the coal mines of south Wales. Both her parents died when she was ten, her grandparents by the time she was seventeen. After that she lived there alone until she married Dan, who came from Pont-rhyd-y-groes, a few miles away near Devil's Bridge. They met when he came as a young man to work on farms in the Rheidol valley.

Dan went on to work first for the railway, then for the Forestry Commission and, for the last twenty-one years of his working life, until his early retirement in 1982, for the Highways Department. Dan and Eirlys are also smallholders, owning a few acres of pasture, and renting a few more, on which they keep sheep. They sell their spare produce, particularly bedding and tomato plants in spring, to help pay for the seed and the heating of the greenhouses.

The garden is a typical one for smallholders. There is a chicken run, a barn containing a jumble of farmyard ironmongery which might come in useful one day, and an elderly Morris Marina Estate in which the produce goes to the show. The soil is kept in good heart, the orderly flower beds are full of cottage-garden flowers, and the vegetable garden is clean, neat and productive. There is even a small orchard of fruit trees and bushes. There are two heated greenhouses, one of which is used for propagation and has a thermostatically controlled propagating unit in it, and another in which cuttings are overwintered and plants grown on. A polythene tunnel shelters yet more. Nothing is wasted: even an old bath, covered by glazed window frames, has been pressed into service as a cold frame for hardening off seedlings. The range of plants sown from seed or grown from cuttings is enormous: pelargoniums, fuchsias, annual chrysanthemums, lavatera, cosmos, begonias, sweet peas, carnations, sunflowers, lobelia, petunias, melons, cucumbers, marrows and tomatoes.

Dan and Eirlys are friendly and welcoming. Dan will sometimes let his wife speak for him but when he does talk it is always to the purpose. He is a deacon of his local chapel. When he retired, he received more than £200 as a leaving present, with which he bought a second greenhouse. He is also much respected and sought out for his horticultural knowledge, which is prodigious. He reads books, takes *Garden News* each week, and watches all the television programmes. (He rather deprecates the slapdash attitude sometimes exhibited on these programmes – watering overhead, rather than putting the pots in a tray of water, for example.) He is careful, methodical and thoughtful.

Although Dan does not come from a family of keen gardeners, he has always grown vegetables and flowers at Cwmrheidol. He attributes his interest to early encouragement from his headmaster at school, who required his students to learn the basics of horticulture. His wife has always been a committed gardener; she remembers helping her grandfather when she was very small. In the garden are a clump of monkshood and a fuchsia bush which have grown there all her life. Her interest lies principally, although not exclusively, in growing annuals, many of which come in very useful for the cut flower classes.

Dan first became interested in showing when working 'on the road.' He laughs when he remembers that he was encouraged by a workmate to enter Taliesin Show in about 1974: 'He had won the cup twice and he was going to win it the third year. And I went and I beat him. He was sorry he told me to come over.'

The Davieses started showing in a small way, just taking dahlias and 'a few things' to local shows, but are now well-known and substantial exhibitors, entering seven to nine shows in a season. Dan also judges in one or two shows a year, but only the flower section. He has been asked to judge vegetables, but he refuses on the grounds that he does not show them seriously so he is not fit to judge them. (This correct, high-minded attitude is by no means universal – which is just as well, perhaps, or many a show would fold from an increasing shortage of available, public-spirited experts.)

At least as far as the garden flowers are concerned, Eirlys is as keen as Dan and much of what they do for show is a joint effort. They like to cut the flowers the night before and plunge them straight into buckets of water. Eirlys arranges the vases of garden flowers that night. She tries not to fill them with too many colours but restricts them to either pink, blue and white, or yellow and tan. She usually wins the class because she takes care over the colours yet includes a wider than average variety of flowers – something which judges appreciate.

It is Eirlys who drives the Marina, with the back seat folded down to accommodate all the produce. It sometimes takes them an hour or so to pack up the car, putting the pots and buckets in bread crates, packed with newspaper and flanked by bricks to stop them sliding about.

Dan is a very experienced exhibitor, but that does not

Mrs Trevor-Jones, the NAFAS judge, closely examines Mary's entry for 'The Pearl Divers' class.

save him from occasionally getting into difficulties. One year, for example, he had had enormous success with his sweet peas, winning everywhere he went with them. But at Talybont Show on the last weekend in August he was disqualified. After the show had opened, the judge asked to see him and told him it was because he had only put eleven stems instead of twelve in the vase; he was very sorry but he had had no option but to disqualify his entry. The same thing happened one year at Capel Bangor with roses. Fortunately his name was called over the public address system before judging began and he was able to rectify the mistake, using one of the spare flowers he always takes with him. These episodes illustrate neatly the attitude of judges at local shows, who find it very painful to disqualify entries on technicalities.

Aberystwyth is the first show of the year for the Davieses and its earliness underlines the importance of the weather. In 1989 their produce was further advanced than usual because of the dry, warm winter and a hot May. Dan hoped to enter two pots of fuchsias, two 'geraniums' (pelargoniums), two vases of pelargoniums 'four blooms of any variety', a flowering begonia, a foliage *Begonia rex*, a variegated succulent, two specimen roses, two entries of four pansies on a board, two vases of garden flowers (including geraniums, delphiniums, lupins, aquilegias, Californian poppies, sweet williams, and monkshood), two entries of six gooseberries, two windowboxes and one entry of four kidney potatoes. In order to have the latter in time for the show he had to grow them in a pot in the polythene tunnel. But the rhubarb which he usually puts in was already finished because of the early season.

Aberystwyth Show is the country agricultural show *par excellence*, too far from any large centre of population to be smart or pretentious, but a very important occasion for all the local farmers, not to mention pony-mad little girls. 1989 saw the forty-sixth annual show held on thirty acres at Tanycastell Park, Rhydyfelin, just south of Aberystwyth near to the river Ystwyth.

When the tent opened at seven thirty, Mary was there waiting to get in and start staging her floral art. The Davieses, Ockeys and other entrants in the 'household' section were not admitted until nine o'clock. Staging could continue until ten thirty and judging started at eleven o'clock.

For Mary, with six exhibits to stage, it was a period of intense, if reasonably disciplined, activity: 'I was very cool, calm, and collected on the day.' 'Down on the Farm' brought Mary's sheep horn into commission, together with foxgloves and heather picked from the garden on Thursday. 'The Good Earth', which had to feature vegetables, gave her a chance to use her alliums (ornamental onions), as well as driftwood, bulrushes, roses, foxgloves and a selection of fruit and vegetables.

Mr Parker, the flower judge, ponders over the cacti in a well-supported class.

'The Pearl Divers' had variegated hosta leaves and white foxgloves. But her *pièce de résistance* was undoubtedly 'Fertility', the modern/abstract exhibit, for which she used her glass bottle half-full with marbles, out of which, from a collar of hosta leaves, shot dyed allium flower heads: 'Like an exploding firework', remarked John Ockey. She also arranged both 'miniature' ('Small Pleasures') and 'petite' ('Twilight Time') exhibits.

In 1988, the winner of the best exhibit in the floral art section (although not the cup, which went to Mary) was Mrs Pixie Harcourt. In 1989 she did not appear until ten forty-five, for she had been delayed milking fifty-two cows before she could come out. Nevertheless, she managed to finish arrangements for most of the classes.

The judge for the floral art was a personage of some consequence in NAFAS circles, Mrs Iona Trevor-Jones from Welshpool. Judging the horticultural produce was Mr Donald Parker, the Superintendent of the University Botanic Gardens in Aberystwyth. Having to oversee a range of glasshouses full of botanical specimens means that his experience is more than usually extensive, even for a professional gardener, a fact which must have pleased John Ockey.

The judges did their work accompanied by most attentive stewards. Mrs Trevor-Jones made her judgements according to a number of principles laid down by NAFAS. Most important is the interpretation of the schedule: the competitors must understand the wording of it, not always an easy matter when schedule-makers have a weakness for titles such as 'Monochromatic Moments'. Then there is the design, that is the picture created by the use of plant materials and accessories (the more original the better), and the scale, that is the relative sizes of materials and container. A good balance is also necessary. It is apparently important that judges do not show any preference for particular colour combinations, just as the judges of the village gardens at Warmington (see chapter 4) will not allow their personal likes or dislikes in this matter to influence them. That said, particular colour harmonies can sometimes help the interpretation of the title.

Even though floral art is not concerned with the growing of plants, but rather their artistic use, judges will downgrade exhibits where the plants are wilting or going over; all must be fresh and clean. As if this were not enough, judges are influenced by how well the design has been carried out technically, for example, whether wire or 'oasis' is showing.

NAFAS does not have a points system, such as exists for the marking of horticultural produce, because it is believed that judges will subconsciously award the points to suit the decision they have already made. But although the competitors do not know, as competitors in a vegetable 'collection' class will know, how the decision was arrived at, they do have the judge's comments to help them. After her deliberations, Mrs Trevor-Jones wrote her remarks about each exhibit in both Welsh and English on a piece of paper for the exhibitor to see.

Mrs Harcourt beat Mary into second place in 'Down on the Farm', 'The Good Earth' and 'The Pearl Divers'. But Mary won 'Fertility' and 'Twilight Time', so despite Mrs Harcourt's Herculean efforts, Mary gained enough points to win the Silver Rose Bowl for most points in the section, even if the Silver Urn for the best exhibit eluded her.

Mr Parker, judging the cacti and succulent classes, had first to check that the pots were in the right class, namely that there were no succulents (without areoles) in the cactus class, or cacti in the succulent class. Then it was a matter of picking out plants which were, if possible, unblemished, of a good size, fitting the pot in which they were planted and, for preference, in flower. Succulents had ideally to have their 'bloom' intact. He was impressed by unusual species. He thought the standard high at Aberystwyth although he frowned on those cacti which 'follow me round the shows' and look rather tired as a result. In the end, in a well-supported class, he gave first to John Ockey's rare and difficult to grow *Mammillaria bombycina*, and first and second to his 'beautifully-coloured' *Euphorbia obesa* and *Echeveria setosa* 'Doris Taylor'.

Dan Davies' industry was rewarded. He shared the cup for the highest number of points in the household and garden produce section. He had first and second for his two vases of flowers, and firsts for his two lettuces and his vase of geraniums. He had second and third for pot fuchsias, second for radishes, gooseberries, and a windowbox, and third for his succulent, four pansies, and one specimen rose. Mary had some luck in this section too: second for one rose, second for the 'shoulder spray', and third for the 'button hole'.

Nearly ten thousand people went through the gates of Parc Tanycastell that Saturday, much to the satisfaction of the organizers. It was perfect weather: dry and warm but not too hot to be oppressive. There were anxious moments, as there always are: the loudspeaker system broke down for a while and the mobile lavatories overflowed but nothing could diminish the pleasure of the Society's officials at a successful day. Competitions went on all day in several show rings, but the highlight was the Grand Parade of winners and the prizegiving, which took place in the middle of the afternoon. The prizegiving in the produce tent was a less exuberant affair, of interest primarily to the competitors and their families. But the entries had been good, and the competition stiffer than usual, so, taken all in all, it had been a good day. So must Mary and Herbert Ellis have reflected as they sat on the tailgate of the car drinking a reviving cup of tea.

Warmington Show in full swing. Jim and Kay Beard amongst the zinnias and dahlias.

CHAPTER FOUR

WARMINGTON

Warmington Horticultural Society's Annual Show

North-east Northamptonshire lies on the belt of limestone which curves all the way from Dorset to Yorkshire. The district's last period of prosperity before now was the Middle Ages, until the Black Death depopulated the countryside. This historical accident has meant that even now the villages are small and modest, though pretty, but dominated by marvellous medieval churches, built of limestone, many of which are visible from a distance across the gently rolling and wooded countryside.

The flatlands of the Fens just to the east are unfortunately no barrier to the cold winds which sweep in from northern Europe in the early part of the year, but sunshine levels are quite high and the rainfall is about twenty-two inches a year, half of that experienced in Dumfriesshire, for example. All this means that a wide range of hardy garden flowers and vegetables can be grown satisfactorily, particularly if there is shelter.

The valley of the slow-moving Nene, pronounced 'Nen' south of Thrapston and 'Neen' above it, has known its share of high drama; the river flows below the site of Fotheringhay Castle, birthplace of Richard III and place of execution of Mary, Queen of Scots. Nowadays the greatest threat to the valley's tranquillity comes from its proximity to Peterborough and the railway line to London. In the last twenty years, even this backwater has felt the wash of progress.

The village to the east of Fotheringhay along the Nene is Warmington, built partly in stone and partly in brick. Until the end of the last war Warmington was still fairly remote and self-sufficient – many of its inhabitants working on the nearby Proby and Fitzwilliam estates – supporting a variety of shops, even a laundry. Even now it has succeeded in retaining its village identity. It is laid out haphazardly, along four adjoining roads, one of which is the noisy Oundle to Peterborough road. Away from that, ducks wander the streets, confident of their next meal from indulgent householders.

Warmington is well known locally for the number of activities in which its population of about 800 engages: adult education classes, the Women's Institute, an amateur dramatic group, and a horticultural society. This last holds meetings and two flower shows, one on the first Saturday in August and the other in October.

The summer flower show has had a continuous existence, except for the war years, since about 1901 (no one is certain exactly when). These days it is held in the village hall under the stare of long-gone football teams, and there are well-supported classes for home-made wine, cookery, floral art, cut flowers (especially sweet peas, gladioli and dahlias), fruit, vegetables, vegetable 'collections' and children's classes. Members of the Warmington Horticultural Society can enter the classes free and do so with some enthusiasm. In 1989 entries were not as high as usual because the hot weather brought the first flush of roses to a premature conclusion.

There is also a village gardens competition. The timing of the judging is kept a close secret, although the competitors make sure that all is in order by the Wednesday evening before show day. This competition is divided into four classes: best garden; best show of flowers in a garden; best vegetable plot, including allotments; and best show of roses in a garden. While the first prize in the show for any single class is no more than eighty pence (apart from 'collections') and is mostly forty pence, the first prize in the garden competition is £1. In 1989 there were eight entries for the best garden competition and 21 entries for all four classes.

For all its range and quality, which is exceptional in a village of such modest size, the present flower show is not the grand affair it was before the war. In those days there was a fair on the village green, a home cricket match, a parade through the village by the silver band and, in the evening, dancing in the marquee to the music of Hancock's band from Oundle.

Sixty years ago, remembers Amy Harbour, whose family moved from a village near Huntingdon to Warmington in 1932 to take up a farm tenancy, the flower show was sufficiently well known to draw people in from quite far afield. It was at the flower show that she met Cyril, whom she married in 1938: 'We were always interested in country life and flower shows and it used to be *the* thing in those days.' In 1941 they came to live at a double-fronted cottage where Cyril was born and his father before him. Half of the house is built of red bricks made in the village brickpits some time in the eighteenth century. The garden has always been a smallholding and extends to about an acre; the Harbours have in the past kept pigs and geese and still have ducks and chickens.

Although well into their seventies, the Harbours are still very spry. Wise, courteous and open without being curious, they are proud of being 'old village'. They love to talk of the old days when no one locked their doors and people depended (and spied) on each other. Although one must resist the temptation to view rural life in the 1930s through the soft focus of nostalgia, the lack of money or material possessions was plainly less important than now, presumably because everyone (except the few gentry who lived in the village and who appear to have been rather philanthropic) was in much the same boat. Allotments, most of which have now gone, were kept as a matter of course, and everyone learned to garden whether they wanted to or not.

Cyril worked for forty-eight years on the Proby estate at the next village, Elton, and was the chief hedge-layer, a job he would do each year from September until March. So good was he that he would enter the competition for hedge-laying, held near Oundle each winter but now defunct. In 1956 he won the championship in a class of thirty and, with it, ten shillings. When first married Amy did not work, except during the war when she 'topped' sugar beet but, later, when their son was growing up, she was a home help to several old ladies in the village.

Although neither set of parents had been exhibitors, both Amy and Cyril were keen from the start, Cyril often digging his vegetable garden after tea in the winter by the light of the street lamp. The Harbours showed only in a small way at first and had little luck because there were so many 'dear old boys', as Amy calls them, who knew the

ropes and were fiercely and jealously competitive. It was hard for the newcomers to gain any prizes. They recall that the other competitors would stand and look at their exhibits in silence but would never tell them where they had gone wrong. Even the technique of growing carrots and parsnips in drainpipes was something they worked out for themselves. This attitude seems to have endured for Cyril, who has had much success with vegetables over the years, says that he never tells anybody what he does in his garden: 'I don't tell them my secrets.' The Harbours had, by 1989, shown for fifty years, although they no longer enter with the same fervour as they once did: 'Years ago we used to grow, more or less, for show . . . but we don't now. If the things are there and good enough they go, but we don't put ourselves about too much.'

At one time sweet peas were a very important element of the Warmington Show, occupying the whole of one end of the wooden hut which served as the village hall until the new one was opened in 1974. No doubt the competition was intensified by the presence in the village of two famous national sweet pea growers, Arthur Dixon and Arthur Oakley. With their retirement in about 1960 this part of the show faded and the cups were transferred to the winners of other classes. This, and aristocratic patronage, are the reasons why Warmington can boast such a fine selection of silver trophies, which the committee still gamely insists on having engraved with the winners' names each year, long after many societies have given up the practice as too expensive.

There has been a gardens competition for many years. Major Geoffrey Bevan, who still lives in Warmington, gave a handsome silver cup to be held for a year in 1950. 'We thought it would be rather fun . . . it was a great success with a lot of entries.' He was keen to encourage the cultivation of proper cottage gardens: it is reported that he did not care for gardens with laid-out lawns like 'seaside promenades'. Major Bevan used sometimes to bring his own judge from well outside the village, and Amy remembers that in the past well-known people would judge the Warmington gardens. He plainly always admired the Harbours' garden because it represented the true cottage garden, with plenty of colour, and a variety of old-established herbaceous plants like poppies and phloxes growing in natural, even haphazard, profusion.

The Harbours' success over the years has been considerable, earning them pictures and reports in the local newspaper. There have been times when it has become embarrassing to them to win the gardens competition so consistently and they have felt constrained to bow out for a year so that someone else's name will appear engraved on the Warmington Perpetual Garden Challenge Cup. They still keep a box full of prize cards: 'I think the most we had was forty – but not all 'firsts' of

course . . . Stupid to keep them, I suppose.'

When the Harbours came to live in the house there was a cobbled yard outside the back door leading to the brick outbuildings. Amy wanted to brighten it up so they built a raised bed, using rubble and stone which they had by them. These days it is colourful in spring with alyssum and aubrieta and filled later with a mixture of annuals like nicotiana, perennials like echinops and geraniums, and shrubs such as roses, both climbing and bush. The soil is manured in October and rested in the winter.

From the yard a flower garden can just be glimpsed through an archway of privet, kept neatly trimmed by Cyril, using not hand shears but a billhook. There is a small lawn beyond, dominated by a large and mature 'Blenheim Orange' apple tree and, beyond that, a thin grass path which runs between two borders of flowers to a wide vegetable garden at the end. In August these borders are a profusion of colour, provided by apricot gladioli, a mass of different roses ('Whisky Mac', 'Peace' and 'Superstar' amongst others) and bedding plants: African marigolds, asters, zinnias and pelargoniums. Backed by old brick outhouses on one side and a row of large shrubs on the other, the colours appear bright

Amy Harbour selecting her gladioli in the flower garden. Behind can be seen the barrier of runner beans which marks off the flowers from Cyril's vegetable garden.

without being strident. So long has the garden been cultivated that it is light and easy to work, yet fertile; like so many village gardens it was roamed (and fertilized) in the past by both swine and poultry. It has been said of the Harbours' soil that if you put a finger in, it would grow. The fertility means that flowers grow well, but the lightness of the soil can be a disadvantage in dry summers. This garden was all put down to vegetables when the Harbours came in 1941 but, as Amy says, she has encroached on it 'bit by bit' over the years to grow the flowers she loves. The vegetable garden is strictly Cyril's preserve.

Amy has always saved as much seed as she can, so much so that the delphiniums, for example, clearly show their larkspur origins. All that is bought are a few packets of seed from the village shop to supplement those that Amy saves: mainly highly-bred half-hardy annuals such as African and French marigolds and asters. Although in the past she did send away for Wheatcroft's and Anderson's roses, many of the roses have either been given to her (there were at one time two keen rose-budders in the village) or grown from her own many cuttings – not always an easy thing to achieve with hybrid tea roses. All the pelargoniums are from cuttings. She has also increased her stock of a very pretty apricot-coloured gladiolus; from an original batch of twelve she now has many dozen, having saved the offsets and planted them out in nursery rows until they were big enough to go into the borders.

The Harbours take pride in their long-accustomed frugality: they use no peat or potting composts but only the soil from molehills. Amy says that the mole has done all the work for her, especially if there has been a good frost. This soil is put in boxes which, after sowing, are put on the house windowsills, there being no greenhouse. They use no artificial fertilizers but depend solely on copious supplies of well-rotted cow manure, which they acquire each year from the farm down the road. This they dig into the vegetable garden and spread all over the garden, but most liberally around the roses. They burn wood in the grate and put all the wood ash on the garden to provide a free source of potash. The Harbours use very few chemicals, from a desire not to waste money rather than strict organic principles, I suspect, although in the clean air they must spray regularly against blackspot. 'Sybol' is used to discourage the carrot fly on one of their most extensively planted vegetables. Asked if they would bother so much if they were not showing, Amy replied that they did not like to see things go wrong but that the show certainly was an incentive.

1989 was a trying year for them: there was a strange virus on the cabbage brought in by greenfly (a plague that year of Egyptian proportions), a frost in late April which took the blossom on the plum trees in the orchard and on the ancient 'Williams' Bon Chrétien' pear on the wall in the flower garden. Worst of all, the near drought and high temperatures in June and July meant that the roses and gladioli came out earlier than usual and the Harbours were worried that there would be little for the judges to see in early August.

Nevertheless, as always Amy would be taking her produce up to the show in the basket of her bicycle (the Harbours do not drive a car). In their younger days, when they showed a great deal, including items Amy had cooked, the small stuff went in the bicycle basket and the rest in the wheelbarrow.

The Harbours have seen changes in how much is required in each class at the show (for instance it used to be twelve beans and peas, now it is six), and also what is shown. Most noticeable is the growth in popularity of floral art. Amy is rather dismissive of the fashion for flower arranging; she thinks it unkind to the flowers. She was well known at one time for her basket of a selection of dahlia varieties but 'years ago it was the *flowers* they judged'. She has not forgotten the year she made up a vase of flowers and a judge wrote on the card: 'Flowers perfect but, oh, why didn't you have a better vase?' 'I didn't see it [the card] soon enough or I'd've written on it "Well, it's a flower show, not a vase show".'

Cheating has always been a feature of flower shows, according to Amy. In the old days everyone grew the same varieties and they minded so much about winning that, if they got the chance, they might, say, swap a carrot with one from the next door dish if it matched theirs better. That is why when exhibitors took the produce to the tent, they had to hand it on a dish to a steward at the door for him to put it on the staging for them. As people care less about these things, so they can afford to be more honest; certainly this practice no longer exists at Warmington, or indeed anywhere else that I have been.

In the course of fifty years of showing, there have obviously been many moments of pure enjoyment. Amy told me a story which made us cry with laughter, concerning the judging of the home-made wine, well-known in the district for both its quantity and quality. 'One year the two men judges, they tasted the wine. One went to sleep and the other couldn't stand up.'

A far more recent convert to showing is Sergeant Bob Brittain, who lives in the police house close to the Oundle to Peterborough road on one edge of the village. Although he and his wife Sheila have always been very keen gardeners, and they have lived in the village since 1976, it is only since 1986 that he has been prevailed upon to show. He is now a real threat to Amy's status as the champion gardener in Warmington: he tied with her in 1987 in the best garden competition and then won outright in 1988, leaving her in second place although

The front garden of the police house. In the round bed are *Salvia* 'Blaze of Fire', *Tagetes* 'Queen Series', the sparsely flowering *Impatiens balsamina* 'Camellia Flowered Mixed' and *Lobelia pendula* 'Sapphire'. Bob and Sheila Brittain try out new bedding plants each year.

winner of the prize for the best show of roses in a garden.

Bob Brittain is everybody's idea of the village policeman: burly, with a ruddy face, a habit of standing with his arms folded, and a policemanly way of talking. He is obviously well-liked and respected on his 'patch', which covers nine villages as well as Warmington.

He comes from a small village in south Lincolnshire and, after National Service, went straight into the police force. By 1989 he had been a policeman for twenty-seven years, with less than three years to go before retirement. He is somewhat envied for his freedom to be off-duty when others are working, and he does not deny that shift work gives him opportunities to garden that he would not otherwise have. However, as he does a forty-two hour week, he is at a considerable disadvantage compared with those who are retired. Most of his spare time is spent gardening, which is impressive considering that the garden does not belong to him and he will shortly have to leave it. He is a very careful and good grower.

The garden extends to about one third of an acre and was well looked after by the previous occupier, one of Warmington's two rose-budders who used to give roses to Amy Harbour from time to time. By the time the Brittains moved in, however, the house had been empty for some while and there was much weed to tackle in the garden. It is now well, though not immaculately, looked after, and full of colour. Bob is lucky that his wife Sheila

is happy to sow a great deal of seed each year to fill the borders with half-hardy annuals. In the early part of the year the Brittains scan the catalogues for interesting new varieties. They also save seed, both of vegetables and half hardy annuals, each year. Box after box is 'set' in March and put either into one of the two greenhouses, or on a windowsill in the house. Amongst the annuals they grew in 1989 were *Lavatera* 'Pink Beauty', *Crepis rubra*, *Dahlia* 'Octopus', *Antirrhinum* 'Sweetheart', *Salvia* 'Hall of Fame' and 'Blaze of Fire', and a selection of marigolds and petunias. They grow a wide range partly because they have found in the past that, if they concentrate their efforts on a particular genus, any problem is disastrous. In 1988, for example, their petunias were attacked by a devastating root mite.

Bob likes to plant the bedding in clumps rather than straight lines 'to get the cottage garden effect', and he favours bold contrasts which is why the central 'penguin pond' in the front garden was planted in 1989 with 'Blaze of Fire' salvias intersected by French marigolds.

There are many fuchsias planted in light shade near a group of trees (for Sheila's uncle is a fuchsia nurseryman), shrubs including a glorious *Clematis 'Jackmanii'* trained over an arch, and a variety of vegetables, both inside and outside the greenhouses, including beans and 'Kelsae' onions. He even grows melons.

There is a small pond (complete with flowing water

The small pond made by Bob behind the house. Part of the vine-covered pergola can be glimpsed in the background.

circulated by a second-hand central heating pump) which he made out of a small wooden boat – he reckoned that if it would keep water out, it would keep water in. But most unusual of all is a vine-covered pergola which stretches across the back courtyard and which was inspired by a holiday spent in Greece. The vine is 'Black Hamburgh' and it originates from his mother's garden, although it has been moved several times. Each September he makes wine with it which he enters in the flower show.

Across the green from the Harbours live Edgar and Barbara Edis, in a bungalow built in 1960. Edgar recently retired from managing the garage in the next village, Elton. Portly and dignified, he now divides his time in the summer between cricket (he is a steward at Lord's and scorer at Oundle School) and cultivating matchless sweet peas. There have been Edises in Elton, from whence he came with his wife and son in 1987, at least since 1574, which is ten years longer than there have been Probys at the Hall. He is much admired for his skill and knowledge as a gardener ('Edgar is very learned . . . he knows all the Latin names', according to Amy Harbour) and his great willingness to help others.

Before the war, when he was a boy, he helped his father on his allotment behind their house, and eventually he and his brother rented their own allotments. His most formative gardening (and showing) influence, however, was undoubtedly his friendship with the two Arthurs, Dixon and Oakley, who were so prominent in sweet pea circles in the fifties. Arthur Oakley, like Edgar, was an 'old Eltonian', and invited Edgar to see the plot that he shared with Arthur Dixon on Broadgate Hill on the outskirts of Warmington. They taught him what they knew about growing and showing. They were breeders of sweet peas, always searching for the (still) elusive yellow flower. Edgar has never taken his passion that far but, nevertheless, is a major contender at Oundle Flower Show, in 1989 winning all the cups and the Banksian Medal for most points in the show. He also swept the board of four sweet pea classes at Peterborough. There is never anyone to touch him at Warmington as far as the two sweet pea classes are concerned.

He does not grow sweet peas for the scent: indeed exhibitors' varieties are rarely as scented as the old-fashioned smaller-flowered 'grandifloras'. He grows them for the beauty of their flowers and the fact that, if tended, they will bloom all summer and into the autumn. They are grown 'on the cordon', that is, each plant is tied to a single bamboo cane, with each sideshoot, second pair of leaves and tendril punctiliously pinched out.

Sweet peas, even those grown 'on the cordon', add to the charm of a garden, something which could not be said about 'bagged' chrysanthemums or covered roses. Edgar would certainly gain points for them in the gardens competition which he entered in 1989, despite his garden not yet being as he would like it. It is a garden in the making and there are areas still to be altered to his satisfaction. He is keen, for example, to make a water 'feature'.

The back garden is divided by a low wall over which alpines spill in spring; beyond are the sweet peas, some sturdy and floriferous dahlias, and a well-kept and productive vegetable garden. Nearer the house are borders of bedding, roses and herbaceous plants, more formally arranged than those in Amy's garden. Next to the house is a long patio densely populated by planted tubs and hanging baskets. A greenhouse shelters perpetual carnations, chrysanthemums and tomatoes. His front garden is showy and thickly planted with roses and bedding plants. He likes colourful borders and thinks they catch the judge's eye, together with some 'feature' and an attractive terrace or patio. It is not, by any stretch of the imagination, a cottage garden, but it is plainly the garden of a skilful and knowledgeable grower.

Kay and Jim Beard came to Warmington in 1984 from Suffolk to live near their married son. Jim is a retired stockbroker and they now live on a small estate of modern houses where once there were allotments and, before that, the brickpits from whence came the bricks for the Harbours' house. Despite the fact that their garden is small they enter the village gardens competition. Kay also makes marmalade and, sometimes, a Victoria sponge which is cooked to the recipe which appears in the schedule. Jim's home-made wine did very well in 1988. Kay is enthusiastic and finds the whole subject vastly amusing; Jim is more restrained but seems just as intrigued.

They have always lived in the country and have owned a succession of large gardens in the past. They are therefore experienced gardeners, with a sophisticated knowledge of plants, and their present garden is beautifully kept and, considering its size, full of colour and interest. Kay aims to have something flowering for twelve months of the year. This is no mean feat in a garden which measures no more than 40 foot by 30 foot. In a mild winter they succeed because they grow hellebores and *Viburnum × bodnantense* 'Dawn'.

The garden is surrounded by other houses, but quite secluded by virtue of the denseness of the fence border planting, which includes many climbing plants. Although the site is almost flat, it is rendered more interesting by a central step and thin low border, which divide the two expanses of lawn. There is an established *Magnolia × soulangiana* 'Rubra' in the centre of one of the lawns, put in by the previous owners, and, in one corner, a *Robinia pseudoacacia* 'Frisia', the yellow-leaved acacia, which they planted over the body of a beloved cat

ABOVE: Edgar Edis pinching out tendrils and sideshoots on his cordon sweet peas.

FAR RIGHT The garden judges, Joe Bellars and Nicholas Warliker, deliberate in Amy's flower garden a few days before the show in August.

so that there never should be any danger of her being dug up. There is even a small fishpond on the upper lawn.

Kay takes great care with the colour combinations and the placing of their summer bedding: pink petunias with blue ageratum, and *Nicotiana* 'Domino' with pink and white lavatera. She does not like regimentation. The air of profusion created by the number of shrubs, perennials and annuals crammed in the borders is fostered by the variety of tubs which stand on the small terrace, which contain lilies, morning glory, even tomatoes. All is neat and tidy, the lawn with sharp edges, the paving swept.

Like many newcomers, the Beards value village life and wish to do their part to foster it. They enter the gardens competition in a spirit of community goodwill rather than any real expectation that they might win. They are, after all, caught on the horns of an increasingly common dilemma, experienced by many village dwellers these days, that of wanting more garden than housing developers are prepared to allow. Jim has managed to rent an allotment, but that was a matter of luck, for Warmington is very short of allotments, now that many of them have been built over.

The Beards chafe a little at the smallness of their garden and believe that it is harder to garden well because there is, for example, no space for a compost heap. They think its size will also militate against their winning the competition. They certainly have never been successful,

but that does not deter them competing 'to support it'.

Judging the village gardens competition in Warmington in 1989 was Nicholas Warliker, head gardener to H.R.H. Princess Alice, Duchess of Gloucester, at Barnwell Manor, a few miles away from Warmington. He is gardening correspondent of the *Northamptonshire Evening Telegraph*, a teacher of adult education gardening classes, and an indefatigable lecturer to W.I.'s and gardening groups. He is without doubt the best-known professional gardener in the district.

He is usually accompanied as judge at Warmington by Joe Bellars, an accomplished showman and former nurseryman from near Peterborough. They have done the task together at Warmington since 1984. Joe is the older man and was not well in the summer of 1989 but, as it turned out, was fit enough in the end to join Nicholas.

In 1989, Nicholas judged twenty-seven shows, which is a great many considering that flower shows have a limited season. His reputation for expertise, reliability and impartiality is such that committees book him as soon as they have had their autumn post-mortem and thoughts turn to next year. 'It is too many in a way . . . But . . . I get a lot of fun out of gardening; I'm putting something back in. It's a bit scary . . . sometimes when I do three [shows] in a day. But I know that I can pace myself accordingly. I won't have to rush myself at one

show to get to another. . . You don't want to appear to be too hasty . . . or too long' If he is too hasty the exhibitors think that he is not really looking at the produce. If too long, the committee are worried that they will not be able to open in time. His most prestigious judging appointment is that of the cut flowers section at Sandringham Flower Show, but he also judges garden centres and town gardens. The most he has done in a single day was forty-six gardens in the nearby town of Corby.

Yet curiously he has never exhibited anything. He feels that, as a professional, if he did not sweep the board in 'open' classes with what he showed, people would say he was not much of a grower; if he did do well, people would say it was only to be expected. However, Nicholas does not see his lack of show experience as a disadvantage, particularly as he often judges with seasoned exhibitors like Joe Bellars.

His remarks about judging chime with much that I have heard from others; there does appear, in this at least, to be a universal experience. Although individual judges have idiosyncracies, they tend to approach their task in much the same way. When Nicholas arrives in the tent, his schedule in hand, he will first look round to gauge the standard and make a mental note of anything outstanding. He then starts with the first class on the schedule and works through methodically, first counting the contents of each dish in case any have to be disqualified. If, taking into account the general level of the show and the season, the standard in a class is not good he may well not award a first prize. If there is one excellent exhibit but the others are mediocre he may not award a second. If he finds that some classes are good, and some are not, people may have put in 'any old thing' for the sake of the points cup, in which case he may not award first prizes in the sub-standard classes.

He sees the RHS Handbook as a kind of Highway Code which should be followed. 'That's not to say that committees shouldn't be writing notes on the schedules for novices.' He finds the RHS Handbook invaluable, even in small shows, and particularly when not judging like with like, as in the cut flower and pot plant classes. Always he takes the comparative difficulties of cultivation into account when judging a class of disparate elements. This also informs his attitude when judging gardens.

Unless gardens are a uniform size, which is very rare – and unheard of in a village – a sophisticated sensitivity called 'using your discretion' is necessary. Nicholas will see old cottage gardens on beautifully worked soils; spartan but fruitful council house gardens; and new gardens made out of fields of the heaviest clay, surrounded by other people's hungry Leyland cypresses. It is, when all is said and done, a matter of personal choice, in a way that judging classes in a flower show is not. After all, people quite properly garden to suit themselves. 'It's the beauty of gardening that no two people's interpretations are exactly the same.'

Despite this, he is not tempted to employ the RHS points system for garden-judging. He can hardly be blamed because it is immensely complicated. 150 points are available: thirty for the general scheme, twenty for the tasteful arrangement, and twenty for cultivation and cleanliness; there are also a variety of categories such as shrubs and trees, and paths, which can attract a maximum of eight points, but only four of these count. Apart from these there is a maximum allowance of sixteen for special features. That is just for the flower garden; a similar system exists for the vegetable garden, fruit garden and the greenhouse. 'I don't like using that; it's too cumbersome and too time-consuming. . . We'd be there all night.'

Instead he and Joe have devised a simplified version with five criteria, each attracting a maximum of twenty points: layout, tidiness, colour (that is, it should be bright and colourful), condition and variety. He has found that, if the exhibitor has a big garden, there will be more variety than in a smaller garden but it may suffer from untidiness. Differences have a way, therefore, of levelling out.

He takes into account both 'soft' and 'hard' landscaping. 'I like to see a "feature", flowers, some vegetables, and even a bit of fruit.' If someone has obviously worked

hard and made a rockery or water garden, what he calls a 'feature', he will award extra points for it because it 'has taken a lot more than just stuffing in a load of salvias.' I pointed out that the house may have changed hands and he may be seeing an inherited feature. He agreed that, of course, you cannot assume that the present owners have done it. But other people get the benefit of generations of good cultivation. The fundamental inequity is just one of those things. I received the impression that, particularly where he had had the opportunity to get to know the gardens, he took all those advantages into account. Nicholas would be the first to admit that judging village gardens is not a scientifically precise occupation, but he obviously believes that by using a points system and 'discretion', it is possible to come up with a fair result. He says that it is not possible to compare as he can by moving three dishes of peas around; 'You can't lift half an acre of lawn up.' What is more, he cannot go back. 'At the end of the time when you leave the garden you've got to make an assessment.'

Perhaps to avoid other traps, he maintains that he is less influenced by good colour combinations than he is by good cultivation; 'I am inclined to ignore colour a little

TOP LEFT Edgar and his matchless sweet peas pose for the camera.

LEFT Cyril and Amy Harbour, competitors for fifty years, discuss the merits of the Victoria sponges.

bit.' It is not that he does not like colour, quite the reverse, but he hesitates about preferring one colour combination over another. It is all part of trying to keep his own preferences out of it. However, he has definite ideas about layout for he would rather see bedding plants grown in drifts than lines and, in rectangular gardens, gives points to those who try to soften the rigidity of the layout. In deference to the examinees, perhaps, he does not take too sophisticated a view of garden design. He certainly has no inherent objection to garden gnomes.

Despite Major Bevan's ambition to foster the indigenous cottage garden in Warmington, Nicholas does not believe that, any gardens, apart from the Harbours', entered in the competition can properly be called cottage gardens. The present day cottage garden, here as elsewhere, is much more likely to resemble a public park in miniature, with modern, scent-less, half-hardy hybrids rather than hardy perennials, herbs and scented climbers. The sophisticated, self-conscious 'cottage garden', laid out à la Margery Fish or Miss Jekyll, with the accent on profusion, old-fashioned perennials and foliage plants, appears also so far to have passed Warmington by.

I asked Nicholas what he did about the fact that he had judged the gardens enough to know perfectly well who owned each one. 'That doesn't make any odds to me.' He knows what is going to happen when he goes in each garden, who is going to tell him what to look for, why

Sergeant Bob Brittain back on duty after the show, the Warmington Perpetual Garden Challenge Cup, for the best garden in the village, in his hand.

they have not done something and what will be out tomorrow, 'but it makes no odds to me because I've no axe to grind.' He judges what he sees and he values his integrity as a judge.

He admits to worrying about judging the Warmington gardens, though. He makes a point of being seen to be thorough; to the extent of dramatizing a bit so that people know that he has been all round. 'Quite often you can cast an eye over something and you're not going to miss much stood in one place . . . But the people would think you'd only given it a cursory glance . . . You know what you're looking for.'

Those who judge at the Warmington Show are asked to be present when the public come in at three o'clock on Saturday, something they may not relish very much. But Nicholas and Joe do enjoy meeting those whose gardens they judge and feel privileged to be asked into their gardens. Nicholas says he would hate to have anybody come into his garden and judge it – he thinks that the exhibitors are very brave. Nicholas enjoys the evident pride some gardeners take in their work and cites the example of the man in Warmington who weeds his lawn meticulously – of the *grass* weeds. 'It's probably the best lawn I've ever seen.'

As a longtime judge he has his share of stories. At one show he was looking at a chamberpot with begonias in it and the handle came away in his hand and the pot broke when he lifted it up to get a better view. He went to tell the Secretary and then he gave it second prize.

At another local show there was an exhibitor who regularly put thirteen raspberries into a class which required twelve. Nicholas and the other judge would tell the steward that they were going to the end of the hall and they wanted to see only twelve raspberries on the plate when they came back. 'I did find out the owner of the raspberries last year and I said "Well, you can't count". It's not in our interest to write NAS over everything . . . the difficulty is if there are only eleven [raspberries].'

At yet another show, 'there were two exhibitors setting up their *Garden News* 'Top Tray' side by side and there was a lot of needle between them.' One of them only put out one cauliflower. 'He was just about walking away from it and the other one's old boy [son] started sniggering. So he thought "Hold on" . . . and he looked and he looked and then it suddenly dawned on him. He should have had two cauliflowers.' So he fetched one from his exhibit for the cauliflower class. He won the points cup by two points, so the cauliflower made all the difference.

The point of flower shows, as far as Nicholas is concerned, is competition and the enhancement of horticultural expertise. What is more, 'you get a lot of mateyness [between exhibitors]. He [an exhibitor] perhaps won't say . . . what that extra ingredient is that he chucks in the bottom of his bean trench but . . . let's face it, if you've won [the beans class] and you give the bloke some of your beans and you beat him again with what you've given him, that's even better, isn't it?'

Barely any rain fell in the two months before the Warmington show. Those gardening on heavy clay, such as the Beards and Edgar Edis, were more fortunate than Amy Harbour with her light soil. The judging was carried out, as predicted, by Nicholas and Joe on the evening of the Wednesday before show Saturday and the results posted on the door inside the village hall at three o'clock that day, as the public came in.

Edgar Edis came third in the best vegetable plot class. Amy was second in the class for best show of roses, which showed she need not have been so anxious about them. But the winner of the Warmington Perpetual Garden Challenge Cup was Bob Brittain, while Kay and Jim Beard earned a Highly Commended.

What impressed the judges was the completeness of Bob Brittain's garden, the harmony between 'hard' and 'soft' landscape, and the range of types of plant grown: climbers, perennials, bedding, vegetables, specimen trees, a vine, even a glade of fuchsias. In comparison Amy's garden had 'no semblance of planning', and, particularly, no 'feature'. Honour was satisfied, however, because even Bob could not beat Amy in the class for the best show of flowers.

Account was taken of the fact that the Beards' garden had no room for vegetables and fruit, but it had a fish pond and a terrace, was thickly planted and beautifully tended. The Highly Commended was awarded to signify that they were not far behind the winners and that the garden had improved since the year before. 'I'm a great believer in encouragement,' was the judge's comment.

It came as no surprise to anyone that Edgar won both classes of sweet peas at the show. In addition, he and the other prize winners earned themselves a picture in the local newspaper. They had all helped to ensure that once again Warmington held the archetypal – and perfect – village show.

Horse-drawn ploughing at the North Somerset Ploughing Match.

CHAPTER FIVE

NORTH SOMERSET

North Somerset Agricultural Society's
Annual Ploughing Match

Apples, particularly cider apples, have been grown for generations on farms in north Somerset, or as it is now rather grudgingly known, Avon. At Long Ashton, a village just beyond Bristol's suburbs, there is even a Ministry of Agriculture research station which, until recently, carried out research work on fruit; indeed it is famous, with the similar station at East Malling, for the development of virus-free fruit stocks. Although fruit is no longer commercially very viable in this area, it is still a good bet for the amateur gardener.

This fertile, favoured, undulating country on the northern edge of the Mendip Hills is the base for the North Somerset Agricultural Society, which began as a ploughing society more than 150 years ago. The Society holds two major events a year, one an agricultural show on the May Bank Holiday Monday (which has been going since 1843) and the other, the ploughing match, on the second Sunday in September. This match takes place on farmland somewhere in the area. In 1989 the match was held at Hill Farm, Barrow Gurney, quite close to Long Ashton. There are several competitions, including ones for such mysteries as 'high cut' and 'semi-digger' ploughing. This ploughing match even attracts horse-drawn ploughs, which is a sight of great beauty and antiquity. The ploughing competition goes on all day, from eleven o'clock in the morning when a Verey pistol is fired, until three thirty in the afternoon when it is fired again. There is also an all-day hedging match, in its own way as ancient and fascinating as the horse-drawn ploughing. There are classes, too, for root crops such as mangolds and turnips, bales of hay and straw, sacks of grain, even ley turf; these are laid out in rows on the stubble close to where the ploughing takes place.

This is not all, however, for in 1987 the show committee decided to institute a crafts and produce tent. This has proved very popular. In 1989 there were 699 entries divided between sixty-six classes. There are the usual flowers and vegetables, but most prominent, not surprisingly, is fruit, particularly apples and pears. The classes are as follows: 'apples, any dessert variety – five fruits'; 'Bramley seedling – five fruits'; 'any other cooking apple'; 'largest cooking apple'; 'pears, any variety – five fruits'; 'plums any variety – five fruits'; 'damsons, any variety – five fruits'; 'blackberries, any variety – twenty fruits'; and 'any other fruit'. In 1989 there were fifty-seven entries altogether, the best so far. With the exception of plums, for which there were no entries (the frost in late April, summer drought and wasps having disposed of most of the local crop), it had been a good fruit year.

Among the entrants for the produce classes was Stephen Patch, full-time gardener at a house in Chew Magna in the Chew valley. He hardly fits the stereotype picture of the employed gardener, for he was only thirty-six years old in 1989. Nevertheless, he talks with some pride and pleasure of working in 'private service'. He became a gardener because he loves the work, rather than from a sense of family tradition. He is a modest man, inclined to understate his capabilities and how much work he does. He was born in Regil, the son and grandson of bakers, but did not want to go into the family business after secondary school, preferring instead to start work as a trainee gardener at Bristol Zoo.

After two years there he left to go to Somerset College of Agriculture and Horticulture at Cannington, where he took the NCH in Commercial Horticulture and later the Advanced National Certificate in Amenity Horticulture. His years at Cannington gave him a solid and extensive grounding. Stephen remembers: 'I always liked fruit but it was one of my worst subjects at college because I could never remember the names of the varieties.' They used to have very difficult fruit identification tests; thirty kinds put out, labelled, for a week, for the students to learn.

After college he went to work in a garden centre for a time, then back to Cannington as Propagator/ Demonstrator for eighteen months and finally into 'private service'. He went to the house in Chew Magna in 1977. When he began working in the five-acre garden there was one other full-time gardener and the retired head gardener who came back to work three mornings a week. Stephen well remembers his comment when he arrived: 'Hah, bloody book-learned, we shall see'. He obviously did see, because they became friends.

Eleven years later his employers sold the house, but Stephen chose to stay with the garden. The present owners are keen on it but have put half of the walled garden down to a double tennis court, which has substantially cut Stephen's workload. This is just as well for Stephen now works single-handed, so that there is plenty to do looking after the pleasure grounds, kitchen garden and orchard – not to mention the flock of woolly and appealing pedigree Hampshire Down sheep.

Showing sheep has become as much a fascination for Stephen as showing produce and his efforts have been rewarded with considerable success.

The sheep were originally bought to help keep down the grass in the orchard and park, which they do quite well, although the trees have to be protected from their appetite for young bark. The orchard consists of apples, pears, plums and damsons, many of them more than fifteen or twenty years old, and some about six or eight years old.

In the kitchen garden there are some established espalier apple trees more than thirty years old, but most of those that now line the garden path are rather younger. Now that the kitchen garden must be decorative as well as functional, the espaliers contribute substantially to the ornamental *potager* effect. Stephen has embarked on a concerted campaign to increase the numbers of varieties grown there, and some of those to be planted in late 1989 were specifically good show varieties.

He has a good range of apples to choose from. There are the dessert apples 'Ellison's Orange', 'James Grieve', 'Laxton's Fortune', 'Charles Ross' and 'Ribston Pippin', and the cooking apples 'Arthur Turner', 'Grenadier', 'Rev. W. Wilks', 'Peasgood's Nonsuch', 'Bramley Seedling', 'Howgate Wonder' and 'Monarch'. Good pollination is therefore ensured. The emphasis on old, rather neglected, but garden-worthy varieties such as

'Peasgood's Nonsuch' is entirely appropriate in this Georgian country house setting, and Stephen has been prepared to travel extensively in southern England to seek them out in specialist nurseries.

The rollcall of pears now reads 'Beurré Bedford' (translated into English by Stephen in time-honoured gardener fashion as 'Berry'), 'Dr Jules Guyot', 'Williams' Bon Chrétien' (pronounced Cretin), 'Beurré Hardy', 'Conference', and 'Doyenné du Comice'. Again, growing a range of varieties ensures a good set of fruit. Plums include 'Belle de Louvain', 'Ouillins Golden Gage', 'Victoria' and 'Marjorie's Seedling'. All are self-fertile. The damson is 'Merryweather'.

The reason for the wide variety grown is the need to provide a variation in season, flavour, and texture to satisfy the wants of the household. Stephen admits that it also helps to provide fruit for the shows. 'Dr Jules Guyot' grown as an espalier, for example, is a particularly good show pear, and 'Belle de Louvain' is a marvellous show plum because of the considerable size of the fruits and their deep vinous colour.

Stephen is disarmingly vague about cultural management of the fruit. They apparently receive a dowsing with 'Growmore', 'and they get on with it'. The 'June drop' does the thinning. Manure is dug into the beds but the only thing which is mulched is the grapevine in the greenhouse which certainly seems to get preferential

treatment; it is carefully pruned in winter and, if Stephen can find time, he will thin the grapes as they grow. He has no doubt that progressive thinning with scissors makes all the difference to the shape of the bunch, the quality of the fruit in general and the size of the grapes individually.

The espalier apples and pears are summer pruned, and the orchard trees pruned in winter if time allows, but Stephen adopts no specific spraying programme for the fruit, partly because of lack of time and perhaps also because he has the luxury of choosing from rather more trees than most people have in a private garden. Although as a result he has some trouble from scab and brown rot, his main pests are greenfly and blackfly on the plums and damsons in the orchard. He is convinced that the quality of fruit would be higher if he did adhere to a spraying programme. The other nuisances are the birds and wasps, if he fails to pick the fruit when it is ripe; but he shrugs his shoulders about these too for, short of putting cardboard covers above picked-out show fruit or enclosing them in muslin bags (as really serious exhibi-

TOP LEFT The flock of woolly and appealing pedigree Hampshire Down sheep which graze the orchard from where Stephen Patch chooses his show fruit.

LEFT Stephen casts a critical eye over his 'Muscat of Alexandria' grapes. He is not entirely happy as the set has not been very good.

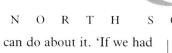

tors will do), there is little he can do about it. 'If we had the staff . . . it would be nice to have a perfect apple and a perfect pear every time on the table, but it's just not practical.'

Not surprisingly, he finds more trouble on the older trees; the young espaliers in the kitchen garden are almost pest-free, no doubt because they are growing vigorously and pests have not had the time to build up into serious infestations. 'Discovery', for example, which is grown on a small espalier, produces one hundred apples every August without fail. The fruits are smaller than the norm but Stephen is not concerned about that. This is a popular apple to show in September because it is ripe (sometimes even slightly over the hill) and judges like to see ripe fruit if possible. (It is not usually possible with most pears which, with the exception of 'Williams' Bon Chrétien', do not soften until after September.)

Stephen finds himself in an impasse; he would like to do things properly for show, but time is of the essence, taking into consideration both the sheep and the garden, so he can only trust to luck. Although nothing is grown specifically for show and he only picks what is available, he is a very keen showman, taking great care with preparation. He started entering at local shows when he was still working at Bristol Zoo: at Winford; Chew Stoke Harvest Home; and the large three-day show held on the Downs in Bristol. He has been as far afield as the three-day show at Weston-super-Mare. He is fortunate to have been born into a region where the tradition of showing is strong, and he has now had plenty of practice at it for such a comparatively young man.

He appreciates that there is a paradox between gardening, which is a reflective occupation, and showing, which is competitive and extrovert, but he is in an honourable tradition of professional gardeners anxious to prove that they are as good as, if not better than, everyone else, despite the many calls on their time.

He is a good loser, however, and is prepared to show slightly sub-standard produce in some circumstances in order to support a show. Having recently helped re-start a flower show at Regil after a gap of some twenty-five years, he is naturally very grateful to those who enter their produce. 'Some of it is not good quality stuff, by any means, but it does help to make a show. Everyone's making the effort.' And he feels obliged to do that with some of the larger shows such as Bristol, Weston and Clevedon. The head gardener ethos – pursuing excellence and leading by example – which was evident around Dumfries is obviously also still alive in north Somerset.

Stephen must enter the shows as a professional gardener, of course, which means that, if the classes are being judged under RHS rules, he has to show in his employer's name. This is because the RHS requires that all exhibits must be the property of the exhibitor and must have been in his possession for at least two months before the show (unless otherwise specified in the schedule). Therefore all exhibits must be entered in the name of the owner of the garden. In Stephen's experience of local shows, no distinction is made between amateur and professional, but he tries to enter 'open' rather than 'restricted' (i.e. restricted to local residents) classes and not to *over*-exhibit at local shows, where he might win most of the prizes just because he has the space to grow a wide variety of things. 'I'd hate to put the local people off, the true amateurs, because [they are] what local shows are all about.' That said, he finds he can be beaten by amateurs growing a far smaller variety of produce because they have the time to be specialists. Moreover, as a conscientious employed gardener, he insists that the house always comes first.

He does not deny that the prize money is useful, particularly if he has to travel to a show, although at the North Somerset Ploughing Match it is only £1 for first prize, fifty pence for second and twenty-five pence for third. Second prizes are only awarded if there are at least four exhibits in the class. At Bristol Show, the first prize is £12 which, as he says, is a prize worth having. He usually comes away from Bristol with about £70, but one year he made more than £100 from twenty exhibits.

Because Stephen enters so many other classes besides the fruit, including flower arranging, herbs, pot plants and cut flowers, he picks the fruit a day or even two days before, taking care with the apples to pick them by cupping them in the palm of his hand and giving a slight twist upwards. He must pick the plums and damsons with the 'bloom' intact, which he does by carefully twisting the stalk until it breaks, and holding the fruits by the stalk until he can put them on plates. When deciding what fruit to pick for the show he may lay fifteen or twenty fruit out on paper plates in order to choose his five, and he will examine them for any fault that may have passed his notice when they were picked. The main problem, apart from punctured skin or blemishes, is finding five of a uniform shape. If he finds that a good pear has lost its stalk he may take one from another pear and stick it in the top, in the rather vain hope that the judge will not notice. The plates are in plastic trays in the shed where they stay until they are taken out of the car and taken in the tent. The grapes travel on crushed tissue paper. He does not wrap anything; he would rather take his chance with them being bruised in order to retain the 'bloom' on the fruit. Some exhibitors might disagree with him about that; indeed many put plums and damsons in cardboard egg boxes to preserve the 'bloom'.

In 1988 he won the 'any other fruit' class with two bunches of the 'Muscat of Alexandria' grape. He showed them suspended on the handle of a basket originally bought for flower arranging but which serves the purpose

nicely. He does not much care for the white-covered boards which are usually produced to comply with the RHS requirement for a stand. He thinks the bunches should be able to hang freely, as they do on the vine. 1989's competition looked like being razor-sharp because the year before two people, seeing his winning entries, promised him 'a run for his money' in the 'any other fruit' class.

Recently, he has planted a 'Black Hamburgh' grape in the greenhouse as well so that in future years (because, of course, it is not ready to fruit yet) he hopes to be able to put in one white and one black bunch. He says he has designs on the grape class at the Autumn Fruit and Vegetable Show at the RHS Halls in Westminster. He likes the idea of competing against the head gardeners employed by the Dukes of Devonshire and Marlborough, who usually divide the prizes between them. The idea of taking these men on – with all their skill and experience – amuses him. Stephen Patch is a man of spirit.

Once picked and sorted, the show produce stays in the potting shed and no one is allowed to touch it. He did lose a couple of shallots once, but not by human agency; veterans of two shows, they were stolen by mice before the third. On another occasion he was entering a great deal of fruit at a large local show, and had decided to leave picking the blackberries until the morning of the show as they so easily become mildewed. The night

before there were guests for dinner in the house and, short of fruit for the dinner table, his employer went out and picked the best of them. Almost in the dark the following morning Stephen picked those that were left, and won third prize, enabling him to win the points cup.

Staging of apples consists of putting four round the edge, stalk downwards, and the fifth standing on top of them, also stalk downwards. The pears, on the other hand, are staged in a circle with the stalks facing the middle. He does the same with the damsons and plums, although he says that many other people line them up in threes. As the North Somerset Agricultural Society only asks for five on a plate, his is the obvious way of doing it.

He takes pride in labelling his fruit correctly, even though he knows that any judge worth his salt will know most of the varieties. It is all part of presentation, which exhibitors fondly believe affects judges favourably. Whether it affects them *that* much is debatable. But, if the RHS Handbook says presentation matters, then it does. Certainly in a close-fought contest the quality of presentation is taken into account by judges. He says it certainly helps the general public.

In 1989 Stephen was particularly busy with the sheep, which were very successful at large agricultural shows, even taking a prize at the Royal Show. Although early in the season he decided to enter most of the fruit classes at the North Somerset Ploughing Match, circumstances conspired to see that it was not possible. There were very few plums and even the grapes were not as good as usual. In the week before the show, he thought he might have to put in a melon instead in the class for 'any other fruit'. Fortunately, the melon is entitled to the same number of points as the grape so his chances of winning the class were not diminished. In the end, however, it was not necessary. Although there were no 'Williams' pears on one tree (probably as a result of the late frosts), he did manage to find some to choose from on one cordon tree in the kitchen garden. That year there was a substantial apple crop, even after the more than usually heavy 'drop' caused by the dry weather in June and July, so he had no difficulty finding sufficient to fill the classes.

Not far away, in the village of Long Ashton, lives a rather different kind of gardener but, if anything, keener and with an even greater range of exhibits to show. Frank Calcraft is a most thoughtful and painstaking gardener, with a justifiable confidence which he masks with a self-deprecating humour. He is not from the West Country, having been born on an isolated farm on the Leicestershire/Lincolnshire border; it was work as a mathematician which brought him to Bristol in 1952, to work on the nascent guided weapons project for what was then BAC. He took early retirement from British Aerospace (as it had later become) in 1987.

Although he had an extremely rural upbringing, his family were not gardeners. However, he knew about fruit grafting by the time the family moved to Long Ashton and, with the natural curiosity of the scientist, thought it sounded intriguing. Most gardeners, particularly inexperienced ones, shy away from grafting; it fills them with justifiable apprehension. Frank, on the other hand, saw it as a 'bit of fun – to make one tree grow a different variety'. He bought a copy of *The Grafter's Handbook* and acquired some apple stocks from a friend who was dabbling in it. He found this technically more interesting than growing cabbages, although he did that as well to help feed his family. 'I should think my successor in that house would have had a bit of a surprise from one tree.' He 'went mad', grafting twenty varieties on it. 'Whether it would have stayed a balanced tree with that lot on, I rather doubt.' I rather doubt, too.

In 1962, not long after they had moved to their present house, which has a south-west-facing quarter-acre garden, the family was posted to Australia, staying there for eight years. As he had just received a consignment of

FAR LEFT Frank Calcraft picking apples for the show from his cordon 'boundary'.

LEFT Frank ponders over which fruit to choose. Ideally, they should be well-matched, unmarked, unpolished and with their stalks intact.

apple and pear trees he had to plant them in a hurry. His trees therefore received only an initial prune and nothing further until 1970. Interestingly enough, he discovered on his return that most looked quite well, and he managed to get several back into shape reasonably quickly.

A boost was given to his orchard in the late 1970s when a new neighbour next door proved sufficiently friendly and garden-minded to agree to the planting of apple cordons along the shared boundary. The cordon is a restricted form of apple tree with one stem which leans, like holidaymakers on the promenade at Scarborough, at an angle of forty-five degrees; it is grafted onto a dwarfing rootstock so that it does not grow a stem more than six to ten feet long. The two neighbours bought and planted alternate trees. Much thought was given to the choice of a good range of cultivars (Frank's neighbour has pears trained 'on the cordon' as well) and, in theory at least, they should start flowering (and therefore fruiting) at the top with the early 'Discovery' and finish at the bottom with the late 'Edward VII'. In practice one tree, as Frank puts it, hasn't read the books and flowers out of turn. He grows both dessert and culinary apples and, although individual cordon trees do not crop heavily, the fact that they can be planted close together means that collectively the harvest is quite good. He grows the cooking apples 'Arthur Turner', 'Idared', 'Grenadier', and 'Edward

VII'. He can boast nine dessert varieties: 'Discovery', 'Epicure', 'Egremont Russet', 'Lord Lambourne', 'Sunset', 'Cox's Orange Pippin', 'Spartan', 'Laxton's Superb' and 'Ashmead's Kernel' – these are names to conjure with. There are also gooseberry and red-currant cordons.

He grows no pears 'on the cordon' because he already possessed three pear trees which survived the Australian interregnum. Despite their lack of formative shaping, they seem to grow quite well, the dwarfing quince rootstock having done its work to limit their size. The varieties include 'Conference', and a September-ripening variety whose name has been lost. These crop well each year because Frank's garden is not subject to late frosts.

He does not grow plums and damsons because where he lives is supposed not to be good 'country' for them. He used to grow an apricot but it flowered so early that it would sometimes blossom with snow on the branches, and there were too few pollinators around at the time for there to be a good 'set'.

As Frank says himself, he dabbles in most things. His vegetable garden is full and various, but there are also gladioli, dahlias (his first love), daffodils which he grows in pots and which he has exhibited nationally, and fuchsias. 1974 was the first year when Frank showed anything – four entries (two potatoes, two dahlias) in the Long Ashton show. 'I ended up with two thirds, because two of the classes only had three entries in them! . . . I knew what I got wasn't that good.' He did it, to see how good, or how bad, they were. He had been encouraged by a retired gardener who lived in the village and was still a local judge. 'He had quite a lot to do with conning me into showing in the first place and in helping me get it better having made a start.'

The next year he had slightly more success but, in 1976, the very hot summer, his knowledge of Australian drought control in gardens paid off and he received his first first prizes – not surprisingly for potatoes and dahlias. In the late seventies he began to go further afield: Portishead, Clevedon, Tickenham, Yatton, and later Weston-super-Mare and Bristol, where he naturally encountered tougher opposition. By 1980 he was also showing soft and top fruit. He took some care with them, he remembers, looking up what was needed in the RHS Handbook in the recommended way. In Long Ashton, the fruit classes were hotly contested: there was a retired grocery roundsman who used to exhibit there who in his time had taken the prizes at the Bristol Show, so the standard was high. The presence of the Ministry research station in the village had a salutary effect on entries too, even if its personnel did not always do as well as might have been expected. No doubt they felt under pressure as the professionals; certainly an invidious position to be in. Frank is treasurer and secretary of the Long Ashton Horticultural Society, which holds a show on the first Saturday in September. He is also a National Dahlia Society judge.

Probably Frank's greatest love is the fuchsia and he is an accomplished exhibitor. He helped to found the Bristol group of the British Fuchsia Society and he is its vice-president and treasurer (it amuses him that people assume he is good at arithmetic because he is a theoretical mathematician). One of his more revealing stories concerns showing fuchsias. He grows half-baskets, which are, in shape, quarter spheres. These are extremely awkward to carry to a show, so he ties two together and puts them on top of a bucket. To this partiuclar show he took a fine specimen of 'La Campanella' and, to balance, an undistinguished half-basket of 'Pinch Me' (fuchsia breeders seem to have a particular weakness for twee names). As 'Pinch Me' seemed more or less acceptable he put it in the class as well. The judge gave him a Highly Commended for 'La Campanella' but 'Pinch Me' won the class! This confirms him in the suspicion that you cannot always judge your own produce, particualrly as judges can be idiosyncratic. He says they get bored with seeing the same thing time and time again. They see lots of half-baskets of 'La Campanella' but rarely one of 'Pinch Me', apparently.

Like Stephen, Frank understands perfectly well about how to look after restricted forms of fruit trees, that is espaliers, cordons, and fans; like Stephen, he also

ABOVE Stephen stages his 'Muscat of Alexandria' grapes.

FAR RIGHT Two fruit experts at work. George Gilbert decides the placing in a well-supported class of dessert apples. The steward is George's late boss, Professor Jim Hirst, retired Director of the Long Ashton Research Station.

practices summer pruning on them to restrict leaf growth and encourage good fruit spur formation. Frank believes in good cultivation with fruit as with all the rest of his produce, although he maintains that there is less that can be done to improve it than with dahlias or chrysanthemums. Like Stephen, he will not admit to doing much extra for his fruit, except perhaps a little thinning after the 'June drop' if necessary. His main problem with fruit, apart from wasps and birds, is cracking of the skin, a physiological disorder probably due to dry soil. He sprays little apart from a tar oil winter wash to kill the overwintering eggs of aphids and suckers, the timing of which is so much less critical than that of the spring spraying programme against scab and insect pests, which is done at bud-burst, green cluster, pink bud, and petal fall stages in order that the pollinators are not affected. Such a programme is particularly difficult for someone who has gone out of his way to plant fruit trees which flower at different times. Perhaps, after all, spraying does not matter so very much if you have a reasonably large range to choose from.

'Compared with all the other things I grow, preparing the fruit for show is one of the smaller jobs . . . If they're on the tree, I simply go and pick them and put them on a plate.' Generally speaking, his pears are not ripe for the August and early September shows, so he simply picks those which are of an even shape and size and

unblemished. He carries his fruit in baskets or boxes with newspaper round them and the individuals wrapped in kitchen roll. He does not leave them out deliberately to 'sweat', as some exhibitors do, but picks them the night before the show. He stages his apples differently from Stephen: he sets four apples round the plate, screws up tissue paper in the middle and puts the fifth on top of that. His pears are staged stalk up.

In 1988 he entered the fruit, vegetable, and flower sections of the North Somerset Ploughing Match and won the cup for the most points awarded in the crafts and produce section.

The unusual climatic conditions of the summer of 1989 meant that the crop of apples and pears was lighter than usual in Frank's garden and no thinning was necessary. Curiously enough, there was little cracking of the fruits, and pest damage (apart from annoying pecks by birds in the necks of pears) was not excessive. No apple grew to a very big size, which meant that Frank was doubtful whether he would have one to put in the largest cooking apple class, but he had sufficient fruit to enter the dessert apple, cooking apple (but not 'Bramley Seedling' because he does not grow the variety), pear, and 'any other fruit' class, this last with a good new autumn-fruiting raspberry called 'Autumn Bliss'.

Stephen and Frank and the other fruit exhibitors are fortunate, for the fruit judge is George Gilbert, Associate of Honour of the Royal Horticultural Society. He is a judge and fruit expert of national standing who has lived in nearby Nailsea since his retirement in 1987 from the Long Ashton Research Station (now the Institute of Arable Crops Research). George is a model judge, the answer to every committee's prayer.

A Cornishman by birth and the son of a butler, George was trained as a gardener partly at Wisley Gardens and from 1951 until 1968 was the Fruit Officer there. Wisley had some 500 cultivars of apple and 150 of pears then and there was, and is, a fruit identification service for members. Between looking after the collection and naming fruit, he could not have had a better training for being a judge. He also acted as a steward at the fruit and vegetable shows held by the RHS at Vincent Square in Westminster. He stayed at Wisley until 1968 when he became the estate and trials manager (Plantations Officer) at the Long Ashton Research Station outside Bristol.

His first judging was done at the flower show at Banstead in Surrey, well known for the quality and quantity of its fruit exhibits, when he was still at Wisley. He could not judge at the RHS's own shows in London because he was one of the Society's officers; however, after his removal to Long Ashton, he began to judge at Vincent Square as well as locally. He professes to enjoying judging but he has been careful not to accept too many invitations because it is such a time-consuming occupation and, for those with a national reputation, can involve a lot of travelling and expense.

George believes that not enough show committees ring the changes with judges, so that once you accept you will be expected to do it again in other years and any refusal after a long time is almost a snub. This works both ways, of course; a show committee can feel that once they have asked so-and-so for several years he will be offended if he is not asked again. So George does enough – one or two local shows and three shows a year in London – to keep his hand in. He is a man of charm, much liked and admired in his profession, his Cornish accent giving him a perfectly justified aura of rural integrity and wisdom. He considers carefully, is fair, helpful, and passionately interested in the whole subject of fruit.

When George is judging there are a number of features he is looking for particularly. One is freshness: he can tell if an apple is going over the hill by squeezing the skin with thumb and forefinger; if it wrinkles at all, the fruit is past its best. Apples are shown 'eye' up, so he must turn them over to see that the stalks are intact. All fruit is shown with its stalks, because bruising can occur, particularly with soft fruit, as the stalks are removed and (although George is too polite to say so) presumably also because it might otherwise have been bought in shops. Stalks should not be cut off with scissors but broken off at the natural place, where the abscission layer has formed. He has no difficulty in detecting when scissors have been used. A mistake that many novices make, he says, is to polish apples for, in all fruit, the retention of the natural 'bloom' is expected. The skin should be without blemishes (anything from wasp holes to brown staining) and with its natural colour.

George is influenced by how people stage their fruit; he is not too concerned about the use of tissue paper or vine leaves but he likes to think that people have been to some trouble to stage neatly. 'It's in human nature' that a judge should choose the well-staged exhibit 'all other things being equal', and in judging there are often, even at local shows, only tiny differences between the quality of exhibits. The decision can be subjective – weighing up a blemish against a bird peck.

Judging can take a long time because George will look over each individual fruit, however many there are on a dish. If, for example, there is a class for a fruit 'collection' – three dishes of three different dessert apples – each dish will be 'pointed' and the points will be noted and left for the exhibitor to see. Even at local shows George will look at every fruit carefully. If there is a well-supported class of, say, 'Cox's Orange Pippin' he judges it by eliminating first those that are obviously not in the running. He takes the card and puts it on the top of the fruit so that he does not have to look at them again and can keep his mind uncluttered. 'You very often find . . . that there is one completely outstanding dish; your eye just goes to it.' He will look at that very carefully for missing stalks or cracked skin before he puts it to one side mentally so that he can concentrate on the other dishes for second and third places.

He also likes to leave a note for the exhibitor if he is forced to disqualify him. He has the same attitude to major infringements whether he is judging at Vincent Square or the North Somerset Ploughing Match. The most common, in his experience, is putting apples in the wrong class: either a 'Cox' in a class for 'any other variety' when there is already a class specifically for 'Cox', or something different in a 'Cox' class. He shows more leniency in local shows however, over the ideal size of fruit and even its freshness, though he admits that judges differ on the point. His view is that if, in a September show, there is a good dish of 'Beauty of Bath', 'Discovery', or 'George Cave' apples which are just past their best, he will nevertheless tend to favour them over unripe specimens of later-maturing apples.

Fruit judges do quite often disagree with each other about freshness, the ideal size, and even about varieties. It is not surprising when you know that there are in existence more than 2,000 apple cultivars and 500 pears.

George himself has disagreed with other most competent judges about the name of an apple. 'Annie Elizabeth' has caused more problems, George thinks, than any other because, if grown on a wall, it can grow out of character. The characteristic 'hammered' appearance of the skin is disguised and it no longer has the density for its size which is distinctive when it is grown in the open. 'I think in the end people had to beg to differ.'

He believes that one of the greatest difficulties that exhibitors have (and some judges come to that) is in accepting that the best dessert apple may not be the largest. This attitude is fostered by commercial concerns who provide big apples for supermarkets, so that some judges who have come from the industry are necessarily imbued with the idea. At Vincent Square he uses apple rings to measure not only the size (the ideal dessert apple is 2¾ inches in diameter, except for certain naturally large-growing cultivars such as 'Blenheim Orange') but also evenness. 'If all other things are equal' (a favourite and typically judicial remark of his), he would give the prize to the smaller apple, provided it were not badly undersized. 'I think this quest for a larger and larger [eating apple] is stupid.' The point of apple rings, incidentally, graded in quarter-inch sizes and opening

Before he judges them, George counts the blackberries. There must be twenty; any more or less will be 'Not According to Schedule' and the entry will be disqualified.

out like a fan, is to prove what may deceive the eye, namely that one apple is bigger than another. Care has to be taken with them, however (and here experience is vital), for some cultivars are not naturally symmetrical, particularly some of the cooking apples like 'Bramley Seedling', whereas 'Charles Ross', 'Peasgood's Nonsuch' and 'Golden Noble' are very round.

Another thing which judges disagree over, apparently, is the amount of colour they like to see on dessert apples. A good judge can tell if an apple has been 'sundewed', that is, picked and put on the damp grass to colour in the sunshine (certainly George has no difficulty detecting that), but some judges definitely favour a more naturally highly coloured apple than others. Colour takes four of the available twenty points, as does 'suitability of size'; condition and uniformity both take six.

The only other aspect that may cause any real problems, according to George, is the class which calls for 'any other variety'. This is put into schedules of larger shows to cater for those not growing the common

TOP LEFT Stephen's 'Williams' Bon Chrétien' are first, followed by Frank's unusual 'Doyenné Boussoch'. The Williams' pears are ripe; the 'Doyenné Boussoch', in Frank's words, 'as hard as bullets in early September'.

LEFT The winners in the 'Any other cooking apple – five fruits' class. Despite being labelled 'Grenadier' when they were really 'Arthur Turner', as George noted, Frank's apples beat Stephen's 'Peasgood's Nonsuch' into second place.

varieties, which will have their own class, such as 'Cox's Orange Pippin' or 'Lord Lambourne'. This 'any other variety' class is often fiercely contested and it takes a strong-minded judge not to feel at least some anxiety about it. George says that judges should not be influenced by personal preference (although it is hard to see how they can avoid it) but should give the prize, 'everything else being equal', to the variety hardest to grow well. 'Cox's Orange Pippin', for example, is a notoriously difficult apple to grow satisfactorily because it is very susceptible to scab and mildew and needs good soil, so well-grown specimens will often find favour in the judge's eye.

Paradoxically, 'any other variety of *fruit*' causes fewer difficulties, because the RHS Handbook is at hand and each fruit will attract different maximum points. For example, at present (although this may be different in the revised 1990 Handbook) melons, nectarines, and 'Muscat of Alexandria' grapes can all score twenty points, but medlars score a meagre five, wineberries eight and figs twelve. Curiously, the grape 'Madresfield Court' and some others score only eighteen, and 'Black Hamburgh', which is commonly grown and sets very well, attracts a maximum of only sixteen. (I am not aware that the RHS distinguishes in the pointing between any other kinds of produce). Aspiring exhibitors of grapes might take note.

He does believe that people need encouraging to show.

He recalls that when he went to work at the research station in 1968, although it was the biggest employer in the village, there was hardly any fruit shown at the local show in early September. 'I couldn't believe my eyes.' He saw to it that the station had a small presence at the next show and for three years after that. His display would consist of three or four labelled dessert apple varieties and perhaps some autumn raspberries. More fruit classes were then introduced and exhibits went up substantially: 'I think you've got to lead by example.' He also used to show fruit from his own garden when living in Long Ashton and had some success with it.

Generally speaking, and despite the unusual strength of competition in the West Country, he believes that fruit growing will always remain too specialized for the general gardener because of the rather offputting pruning and spraying routines, the need to have a favourably placed garden and the need to understand rootstocks and pollination. It is no coincidence that those who show fruit are usually very keen all-round gardeners such as Frank Calcraft and Stephen Patch.

George must take some of the credit for encouraging the showing of good quality fruit at the North Somerset Ploughing Match. The show organizers went to him for advice about the fruit classes when the produce tent was established in 1987, and it was his idea the following year to introduce a largest (in circumference) apple class, 'for

fun and to create a bit of interest'.

In 1989 he was asked to judge again, and the steward accompanying him was his old boss, Professor Jim Hirst, retired Director of the Long Ashton Research Station. They assembled for their work after the 'Blessing of the Plough' service held from a trailer by the rector of Barrow Gurney, Peter Wills. The day was grey and cold. The long hot summer of 1989 was finally over.

George was impressed by the quality and variety of the fruit, in particular the dessert apples, of which there were twelve entries. After a great deal of deliberation, he gave first prize to a dish of ripe 'Ellison's Orange', which he discovered later belonged to his doctor. 'I told him that I couldn't smell them properly [the apple has a distinctive aroma of aniseed] because of my sinus trouble!'. Second was 'Laxton's Fortune', also ripe, shown by Stephen Patch, and third 'Spartan'. There were two reserves, because it was such a strong class: 'Sunset' shown by Frank Calcraft and a 'Cox's Orange Pippin'. 'You've got to be hard on yourself and not automatically go for the 'Cox' because it's harder to grow well; those I was judging were not particularly well-coloured and the fruits were rather small.'

Stephen Patch's 'Bramley Seedling' was third in a class of eight, and Frank's 'Arthur Turner' took first in the 'any other cooking apple' section. He accidentally labelled them 'Grenadier' but George put him right; the mislabelling made no difference to the placing. Stephen was second with 'Peasgood's Nonsuch'. Stephen's dish of 'Williams' Bon Chrétien' pear found enormous favour with George; it was followed by Frank's unknown pear. George tentatively identified this as an old variety called 'Doyenné Boussoch' not grown much any more, but said he needed a second opinion.

There were three damson entries, proving that this is a hardier stone fruit than the plum. Stephen's 'Merryweather' won the class, but 'we had to search round for a good "five", for there were only twenty or thirty fruits on the tree'. In the 'any other fruit' class, however, Stephen's 'Muscat of Alexandria' grapes won, even though, as he cheerfully admitted, they were not as good as they might have been. George would have agreed. He preferred an excellent, thinned, well balanced bunch of 'Black Hamburgh' which was second but, because the 'Muscat' commands more points than the 'Black Hamburgh', it won the class. The points were seventeen out of twenty for the 'Muscat' and fifteen out of sixteen for the 'Black Hamburgh'. Frank's autumn raspberries were unplaced.

Although Frank won several first prizes for vegetables, the cup eluded him this year, going instead to a wizard cook. As all experienced, and therefore philosophical, exhibitors say at the end of the season: 'There is always next year.'

Three RNRS judges deliberate over the 'box of six' class.

CHAPTER SIX

LAKELAND
The National Northern
Rose Show

A consistent feature of all summer flower shows, large and small, is the rose class. Every interested gardener grows roses and, however amateur or reluctant, he or she can usually be persuaded to pay ten pence to enter, squeeze a few hybrid teas of indeterminate variety into a vase, and hope for the best. But the modern bush rose (that is, the hybrid tea and the floribunda) is, together with the chrysanthemum, the dahlia, and the gladiolus, one of the great and enduring exhibition flowers, with a sufficient following to warrant its own annual National Championship, run under the auspices of the Royal National Rose Society. So, lest the reader should form the impression that all showing is cosily informal, and as social as horticultural, I went to the north-east of England to meet two men for whom exhibiting roses is a way of life.

Don Charlton and Tom Foster are often called 'professionals', a misleading term given by casual show-men to those who see exhibiting as a serious business and who compete at national level. They are not professional in the sense of making a living out of what they do; rather the reverse, for rose-showing at this level is an expensive pastime, involving considerable travel, overnight stays, and the acquisition of a large car. The financial rewards are larger than can be expected at local shows but still bear no comparison to expenses incurred. Don Charlton competes in the 'open' classes because he possesses more than 1,000 rose bushes (the average garden has no more than twenty or thirty.) Tom Foster owns a more modest 500 and enters those classes which are for 500 or fewer, although he can compete in the 'open' classes as well. There are also classes at a national level for those with a maximum of 250 and 150 bushes. Don has been National Champion eight times, while Tom has been the '500s' Champion seven times. They are firm friends and even share a garden in Billingham, near Middlesbrough.

Don is the more voluble of the two men. He talks articulately and at length with a considerable recall of events and particularly rose names. He is single-minded, seemingly incapable of the vitiating self-doubts which would fatally undermine the serious exhibitor, but one gets the impression that his present self-confidence has grown with success and is not innate. He and his wife, Jennie, who is also passionately keen on roses, live in a quiet corner of Billingham-on-Tees, ICI's company town, in a house they acquired in 1960, soon after Don joined ICI. He took early retirement from his job as Shift Controller in the Research Division in 1986. These days, apart from growing his roses, he takes adult education gardening classes, lectures locally, conducts judges' seminars for the Royal National Rose Society, judges at rose shows and acts as an inspector for the RNRS's regional rose garden at Redcar. He is chairman of the Teesside Rose Society. The Charltons are outgoing and burningly keen to encourage anyone who is at all enthusiastic about roses.

Don's father was a miner from Shotton in County Durham who went to some lengths to dissuade his grammar school-educated son from going down the pit. He succeeded and, although young Don worked for a time for the National Coal Board at Castle Eden, he soon moved on to the docks at Middlesbrough and later to ICI. His interest in gardening really began when he settled in Billingham, but he remembers as a very young man cycling to work through the village of Castle Eden and being struck by a colourful cottage garden, full of roses. He would stop to talk to the cottagers and discovered that the roses all came from McGredy's in Northern Ireland. The impression remained with him; when he acquired a garden he sent to McGredy's for roses, which still grow, after nearly thirty years, in the front garden.

One day in the early 1960s, his father, on a visit to his son's house, noticed that the roses were at their best and took away an armful to exhibit at Easington Flower Show. So successful was he with them that Don was encouraged to have a try himself. There was then, as now, a strong tradition in the north-east of growing very large 'pot' leeks and onions, which even in those days could win prizes of £100 or more. Don shied away from growing them, however, because of what he considered the cut-throat nature of the competition. Stories of rivals throwing handfuls of nitrogen-rich sulphate of ammonia followed by buckets of water onto other gardeners' leek trenches, causing the leeks to split, were common then, and such dirty tricks repelled him. It would hardly have appealed to a man so prepared to share his knowledge with others that he has written a book about exhibiting roses (*Growing and Showing Roses*, David and Charles, 1984). Roses, which attract comparatively limited prize money seemed to offer all the opportunities for showing skill in growing without the unpleasant rivalry which can occur when substantial sums of money are involved.

As a new gardener Don grew a variety of flowers – chrysanthemums, fuchsias, sweet peas – which he showed locally, despite his having only a very small garden and an eight foot by six foot greenhouse. Then he managed to borrow a plot of land nearby which he shared with a keen fuchsia grower and, between them, they put on substantial stands of fuchsias and chrysanthemums at local shows. He abandoned indoor chrysanthemum showing, however, after he discovered that his entry of five 'Beacon' chrysanthemums was competing in a class against five of his own flowers (he remembers them as a white incurved variety called 'Far North') which he had put in a 'sales class' the day before. (A 'sales class' consists of entries which are not taken back by their owners after the show but sold to raise funds for the society or a local charity.)

He turned more to sweet peas and particularly roses, and had considerable success with these at local shows. One of the reasons Don chose roses was because they do not last a long time in their prime; even the many-petalled varieties will only last for about forty-eight hours if they are picked at their peak, unlike chrysanthemums which will survive up to ten days so that the same flowers may appear at more than one show. Some roses are of such fleeting beauty that they are only at their best for twelve hours, so that he considers it a great challenge to present them in perfect condition on the showbench.

However roses do have two flushes of flowers, which means that it is possible to compete several times in the course of the summer. He also believes that roses lend themselves to staging.

He soon found himself taken aside by judges and told that his flowers were of sufficient quality to stand more taxing competition. He became more selective about the varieties he grew and joined the Teesside Rose Society, meeting for the first time very keen rose exhibitors such as Tom Foster.

He remembers that the older exhibitors tended to keep what they knew to themselves, but that there were younger men prepared to talk about showing. 'It was the days when all the big roses which were presented were almost strangled with rose ties around their centres; although very large, they were wan, pale, and old, and I used to think that there was a better way to do this, somehow.'

Encouraged by two women members of the Teesside Rose Society who forged his signature on an entry form because he was so reluctant, he found himself showing roses at the Northern Show of the RNRS at Roundhay Park in Leeds in 1974. He had been entered in the 'B' division because he was then only growing 650 roses. 'They actually carried all the exhibits to the bench as I was a little overawed. And, although I was following the schedule, I didn't really know what I was doing' – which

is hardly surprising, for national schedules are daunting in their complexity. The roses won eight prizes.

That was his entry into the big time. The following year he exhibited at the Lakeland Rose Show, which as well as staging the Lakeland Championship also incorporated the National Northern Rose Show of the RNRS, the show in Leeds having folded. It was therefore one of the three shows where points could be scored towards the National Championship. He was competing against those growing up to 3,000 bushes, despite having only 750 bushes to his name, yet he won the Lakeland and Northern Championships: 'Probably the most exciting rose day that I can remember.'

By this time, he had been lent two more pieces of ground in Billingham, the largest being something under a quarter of an acre behind a house in York Crescent. It was too big for his needs so he asked Tom Foster to share it with him.

Tom Foster is much the same age as Don, very softly-spoken and less ebullient, but just as hard-working and knowledgeable and, if anything, even more single-minded. He and his wife Iris live in the seaside village of Seaton Carew, near Hartlepool, about five miles from

LEFT Only individual 'blooms' can be protected. Note the glossy perfection of the leaves. The rose is 'Die Welt'.

RIGHT Don Charlton cutting floribundas the day before the show.

Billingham. They run a thriving fish and chip shop business. Tom is also very competitive, having taken up rose showing when he gave up playing match cricket (in his prime, it is said, that he was a ferocious batsman who, at charity matches in Yorkshire, could hit Fred Trueman's deliveries around the ground). Tom, like Don, worked unsocial hours, so there was often time in the day for tending roses.

At that time Tom was having trouble in his own garden with 'sea frets' (mists which come in with the tide), which were spotting some of his roses when they were under protective covers, so he and Don agreed to halve the plot, more or less. For two months, from September to November, they worked twenty-seven hours a week double-digging the ground to make it ready for planting. 'That's how we became really friendly' says Tom. He believes that there is nothing better to cement a friendship than being on your knees together pulling out weeds by hand. They were then, as now, scrupulous about keeping the roses that they owned separate and cultivating their own plots; the only time they break that rule is when Don sprays 'Nimrod-T' against mildew and blackspot, because Tom is allergic to it. The friendship which has grown up between them as a result of their sharing this piece of ground has plainly had enormous benefits for both. Their conversations have resulted in the development of a sophisticated crate system for carrying roses and also introduced the plastic bag and polystyrene cup as bloom protectors to the rose exhibiting world.

By the time Don met Tom the latter was well established as a local showman. Gardening had taken hold of him in 1969, when he bought a few roses from Wheatcroft's, and also some dahlias. Two years later he acquired a greenhouse. Until then most of his spare time in the summer had been spent on the cricket pitch. It was at a cricket match, fortuitously, that he met a journalist from Hartlepool, who was both a keen cricketer and a rose enthusiast. Bill Ellerker wrote a weekly article on gardening in the local newspaper but his favourite subject was roses; he advised Tom to join the Royal National Rose Society.

At that time, Tom was friendly with a well-known chrysanthemum exhibitor who lived quite nearby. Tom went to see his garden and was amazed at his dedication. He felt inspired to show – but not chrysanthemums. He was rather put off by the attitude of certain local growers who would pool their chrysanthemums to show against his friend because he was an exhibitor with a national reputation. Tom put it down to the money that could be won in showing chrysanthemums, which might well be as much as ten times that for exhibiting roses in local shows.

He felt he wanted to show something because he had

finished with football and was now coming to the end of his cricketing career. 'My competitive urge had to come out somewhere.' His first essay into showing was not successful as he had no idea how to transport roses safely. However, noting the care his friend the chrysanthemum grower took to see that all the stems were tied individually in the crates to prevent any petal bruising, he devised a system which he could operate on his own, using washing-up liquid bottles, with their tops cut off, wedged in bread trays. He also took note of how much time his friend spent 'dressing' his blooms at the show.

Not long after, probably in 1973, he joined the Teesside Rose Society, which was when his and Don's paths crossed for the first time. The following year Tom, like Don, swam out into deeper waters, competing at the National Northern Show in Leeds.

1976 was the centenary year of the Royal National Rose Society and incidentally one of the few years, as Don says, 'when we couldn't complain about lack of sunshine'. The first of the three shows where points could be gained for the National Championship was held that year, not at the Society's gardens near St Albans, which is usual, but at the Horticultural Halls in Westminster, and it was one week later than usual. That fact undoubtedly helped the northern exhibitors, who often have no roses fully out in time for the first show, usually held on the first Saturday in July.

Don and Tom decided to travel together. They packed 220 'blooms' into special crates in the back of Tom's Volvo Estate and drove south at night, staging their roses when they arrived. Don remembers that, as he sat in the car coming into London, he sketched a diagram on the back of a matchbox of how he would stage the bowl of eighteen roses, different varieties, for best effect: seven at the back, six in the middle, and five at the bottom.

Staging that day was an experience which left an impression on them both; they felt rather overawed – a couple of comparative novices from the unfavoured north-east. After the judging was over, Don and Tom returned to the hall and Don went immediately to the bowl of eighteen roses. 'In front of it were two gentlemen in white linen jackets (I had never realized that judges attend summer shows in linen jackets). . . They said that the centre rose, an 'Admiral Rodney', had been chosen as the best rose in the show.' In all he won five or six first prizes and the Teesside Rose Society won nineteen firsts. 'We came away in a pink haze.' (I have seen a photograph of Don's bowl of 'eighteen' reproduced in more than one book as an example of how best to stage that particular number of roses.)

The following week the northerners had little to show for 'Lakeland' as it is always called, the first flush of flower being quite over, but the Charltons and Fosters went all the same and Don managed to accumulate a total

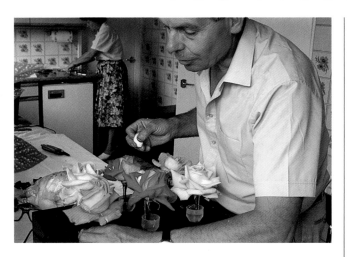

of 4¼ points for the whole show. Tom fared little better. Despite this, Don was pressured by friends to produce roses for the Great Autumn Rose Show because there was an off-chance that he might win the National Championship. There was, at that time, only one National Championship, for not until the following year was one established for competitors with fewer than 500 bushes. But Tom went to Westminster anyway.

All through that droughty summer they saved their waste water for the roses and even sprayed them twice a week with a foliar feed because the roots could take nothing up in the dry soil. They went to the show in Westminster in September. The competition was very

close and, after a lot of discussion over points, the result was put up on the pillar as a win for Fred Owen, National Champion the previous year. Half an hour later, the result was changed to a draw between Fred Owen and Don. Don received a letter the following Wednesday from the RNRS to say that he had won. Fred Owen had meticulously tallied all the points and discovered that the Society had made a mistake. So Don won by a quarter of a point. Fred told him in the Hall that the RNRS had made a mistake and bought him a pint after the show.

Don had won the National Championship when competing for the first time at national level, and with it a centenary silver medal. 'The other thing I was overjoyed about was that, at the Autumn Show, Tom produced a magnificent 'Fred Gibson' in his vase of "six" and was awarded a silver medal [for "Best Bloom in Show"]. So two out of the three silver medals came to the north-east.' 'I was absolutely over the moon', said Tom. 'I've won five or six "Best Blooms" since then but nothing's been like the thrill of that first one.'

Many people ascribed the success of the north-east rose-growers that year to a quirk of the weather.

ABOVE LEFT Don 'dressing' the roses in his box of 'six'. He uses a different colour cotton wool to that of the rose, so that he will not forget to take it out at the time of staging.

RIGHT Jennie Charlton ties a selection of hybrid tea roses into the travelling crates. Each one is in its own container of water.

Certainly the following year Don and Tom did not even have roses out in time for the Lakeland Show in the middle of July. However, in 1978 Don came within four points of taking the National Championship, and in 1979 he won it. Up until 1989 he had won it seven times more. Tom was the '500s' Champion seven times in the twelve years that it had been in existence. Their supremacy had not yet been successfully challenged.

Tom says he still feels as excited as ever at the beginning of the season, except when the first show is too early for their roses to be out, so that winning the championship is made very difficult indeed. They have occasionally missed an autumn show, too, notably the year when a gale brought a large tree down on the roses.

While Don is very keen on most aspects of the 'rose world', Tom is only really interested in exhibiting. 'I'm a different kettle of fish from Don. I'm a competitor'. After much badgering, however, he was prevailed upon to take his judge's exams in 1989; until then he believed that judging would get in the way of showing. 'Everything I do, I've got to try and do well. . . No half measures.' Certainly after half a night of staging, having to put on an RNRS tie and judge a section of exhibits must take determination.

Roses are grown for show much as they are grown in ordinary gardens, except more so. That said, if you intend to show them, there are four very important factors of which you must take account. The first is timing of pruning and spraying, the second is disbudding of the flowers for size, the third is protection of the flowers (or 'blooms'), and the fourth is choice of cultivar.

Timing is as scientific a technique as is possible when so much in growing depends on the weather. There are some general indicators, however. For example, floribundas (or 'cluster-flowered roses' as they are now properly, though not yet widely, known) take longer to flower from pruning than hybrid tea roses (correctly, but clumsily, 'large-flowered bush' roses). So floribundas must be pruned in late February, whereas slow-to-flower hybrid teas are not cut back until early March and quick-flowerers even later. The idea is to have plenty of roses ready for early July, but the weather can make a difference of three weeks either way. How hard they are pruned depends on variety and how much frost damage there has been. Some shoots are cut harder than others to stagger the flowering time of the bush.

Disbudding is not something that the ordinary gardener concerns himself with very much. If he wants large flowers he will prune to three or four buds from the ground (four or five in the case of floribundas), but he is very unlikely to snap off either the side buds or those growing from the leaf axils of sideshoots as they develop in early June. Only the real enthusiast does that.

Protection of the blooms is obligatory for the show exhibitor, particularly because roses tend to have many petals and so suffer badly in the rain. (This is why some show roses like 'Red Devil' and 'Big Chief' are so rarely seen in ordinary gardens.) However, only covering of *individual* flowers is allowed by RNRS rules; unlike chrysanthemum growers, rose exhibitors are not permitted to stretch a cover over the entire garden. Obviously, floribundas cannot be covered; fortunately many stand the weather well. What governs the choice of floribundas for show is truss and flower form and whether they retain their colour well. In the past, rose exhibitors fixed plastic cones onto canes or adjustable stands which they set above the hybrid tea flowers as they opened. These are no longer commercially available, so exhibitors make their own. Don and Tom have a mixture of old commercial plastic cones which, for some reason, are a lurid red or yellow, and some they have made from stiff cartridge paper covered in waterproof paint. The result is not pretty but, as Don happily admits, theirs is not a garden but a rose factory.

Plastic cones are not ideal in any event: they can swing about in the wind, they are time-consuming to erect and their height must be adjusted as the rose grows. Tom, particularly, found that plastic covers did not do well at Seaton Carew because of the strong winds and the 'sea frets'. He tried greaseproof bags from his shop, similar to those which chrysanthemum exhibitors use, but they were too unyielding. Then, in the hot summer of 1976, thrips were an enormous nuisance because they spotted the petals, so Don suggested that they try clear plastic bags (even though they had always understood that these made the roses sweat) because the roses were going to be lost anyway. By trial and error, the two men discovered that the bags worked well with most roses except for some of those without many petals, such as 'Red Lion', or 'Grandpa Dickson' which grows too fast, provided that the bags were removed every two days, turned inside out and the drops of water shaken out before being replaced.

The technique is simple; the bag is blown up like a balloon, put over the rose bud as it begins to colour up (which is when the neck has stiffened sufficiently to hold both flower and bag without bending), and then tied at the neck using a paper tie known by them as a 'twist-it'. The bag acts as a miniature greenhouse so can be used to hurry along tardy buds, but it has to be taken off by the time the rose is half-open or the bloom will go past its best too quickly.

A year or two later the men were finding, for some reason, that many of the 'Red Devil', which is one of their 'banker' roses vital for show success, were producing sunken rather than high centres. They discovered that by tying on twelve-ounce polystyrene cups (of which

Tom had an almost endless supply in his shop) when the stems were firm, they could encourage the centres to grow up much better. They discovered that it was a good way of protecting the blooms of many other roses. These polystyrene cups are cheap, quick to put on, lighter than plastic cups, do not produce condensation inside, let in light, yet are heat-insulating and do not induce facing of bright colours. Don believes that they are probably the best answer for the ordinary gardener who wants to grow a dozen decent roses for the village show.

The cups will not blow off because the men have

Tom takes out the cotton wool from the roses in his 'box' of twelve 'specimen blooms', while his wife, Iris, checks the schedule. The reason for the apron is clear.

devised an ingenious way of tying them on: they make four holes, two on each side of the cup, so that the 'twist-it' can be poked through and across to the other side. Because the cups are flexible they can be put on in a hurry, and the chaps keep a supply ready, with 'twist-its' attached. The disadvantage of polystyrene cups is that they do blow around in strong winds, which can bruise the petals. They also have to be removed before the rose is fully developed or it may be damaged. Such techniques demonstrate how endless is the refining of skills; these men are always on the lookout for ways of improving what they do. I have no doubt that therein lies much of the secret for their continuing success.

The fourth aspect of showing is the very careful choice of cultivar. Over the years exhibitors have established a list of show roses, called 'bankers', which may or may not be seen regularly in ordinary gardens. Varieties like 'Admiral Rodney' and 'Gavotte' are rarely grown, whereas 'Silver Jubilee' is in the garden of everybody who has been married for more than twenty-five years. In general terms, though, showmen's roses tend to have large flowers and many petals, which means they are inclined to ball up in bad weather and will not open properly. They must be pampered to perform well.

The showman is fascinated by the classic form of the hybrid tea rose – circular in outline, with a regular, conical, high-pointed centre, with outer petals which reflex as they age. For this he will tolerate with equanimity the stiffness of the bush's shape; in anticipation of summer beauty he barely notices the dreariness of the rose garden in winter.

The season's campaign for Don and Tom starts at the end of October, when the roses are cleaned up, any flowers removed, and the bushes cut back by about a third to prevent windrock, which can cause damage to the roots by allowing water in at the stem which will freeze in winter. Towards the end of the year any leaves which have not already fallen are removed, because they carry the danger of fungal diseases like black spot and rust.

In January, if the ground is not frozen, a soil conditioner is applied. 'People think there are magic potions to put on the soil.' Don disagrees but he does use powdered seaweed, 'Seagold', not as a feed but because it will improve the crumb structure of any soil, and heavy clay particularly. He has carried this out for several years and has really improved the soil. His soil is a medium-heavy loam with clay below about fifteen inches. It is ideal for roses. The pH is about 6.8 – which roses like. '"Seagold" is naturally buffered about seven anyway' (which demonstrates that Don knows rather more science than is usual amongst gardeners). 'It does contain trace elements which do enhance colours.' Don's years of working for ICI have been a great help to him; he is quite

at home with the scientific aspects of growing. He corrected my mistaken belief that Billingham would be a good place to grow roses because the sulphurous smoke, which appeared to pour from the chimneys nearby, must discourage blackspot. Apparently the emissions are now so clean that it is necessary to spray against the disease.

No pruning is carried out until the end of February. Because the flowers of floribunda roses take longer to develop, they need to be pruned earlier than hybrid teas. Fortunately, most of them are hardier. There is then a short gap of two weeks during which time the men acquire their substantial supply of well-rotted farmyard manure which has to be brought into the gardens in some 150 large bags. The first hybrid tea roses are pruned from about 7th March, when the worst frosts are usually over. In 1989, because the winter was so mild, much of the premature new growth had to be cut out, but that did not seem to have any effect on the flowering.

Once the pruning of the hybrid teas begins, the varieties which take longest to develop, such as 'Red Devil', 'Big Chief', 'Bobby Charlton', 'Die Welt' and 'Doctor Dick', are chosen first. About ten days later the mainstream cultivars like 'Royal Highness', 'Bonsoir' and 'City of Worcester' are pruned and finally, ten days after that, it is the turn of 'Grandpa Dickson', 'Gavotte' and 'Admiral Rodney'. All roses are classified according to the length of time they take to develop from pruning to flowering. This classification can only really be done by experience, although there are lists available. Miniature roses are not pruned until the first week in April.

Immediately the pruning is finished, a topdressing of slow-release fertilizer (four parts 'Enmag' to one part 'Gold N') is applied at a rate of four ounces per square yard. The alternative is 'Vitax Q4' or, after a very wet winter when the nitrogen has been leached out of the soil, 'Vitax Q4HN' (which is high in nitrogen). If, as happens, they cannot get hold of 'Gold N' they put on ICI's 'Rose Plus'. They always scuff it into the top inch of soil. Then they apply a mulch – well-rotted farmyard manure to a depth of two to three inches.

After about six weeks the roses have started to make new shoots. These buds are gradually reduced, until there are only two on each stem. As exhibitors space their roses closely, that reduction may have to be even harsher, leaving in the end perhaps only five or six buds per plant. 'Those are the hard moments when these beautiful stems have to be cut off.'

As the leaves are developing, a spraying programme is begun. Tom and Don use an ICI product 'Roseclear', (which is recommended for blackspot, mildew and aphids but does not kill lacewings or ladybirds) which they alternate with the fungicide 'Nimrod-T', another ICI product. (It is obviously hard to break the brand loyalty of a lifetime.) This spraying continues every ten days right up till the time when the flower buds are beginning to show colour, usually about the end of June.

Feeding consists of applying a granular high potash fertilizer on top of the mulch when the first flush is nearly over. If there is no rain, this is watered in so that it reaches the roots. This application is usually sufficient to last until the autumn.

Occasionally specific varieties receive special treatment, notably one or two applications of iron, usually 'Maxicrop' with added sequestered iron, mixed with water to make a liquid feed. 'Grandpa Dickson', 'Royal Highness' and 'Admiral Rodney' are the most likely recipients. 'I am convinced that potash and iron are the main elements which give us the extra deep colouring to the petals.' Foliar feeding is only practised if the soil is too dry or too wet for the roots to function properly.

Disbudding is begun in June. The side buds of hybrid tea roses and the truss centre buds of floribundas are snapped off to allow the others to develop to a greater size. After that it is a matter of protecting specific blooms from rain and strong sun in the run-up to the day before the show. The trick to this is a methodical approach and being prepared to go round the rose gardens at least every other day. In reality, Don and Tom spend most of their time in the gardens in the last weeks of June and the first of July. In 1989 the auguries were good. The unusually mild winter and hot summer meant that there was going to be plenty of flower in time for St Albans, indeed some roses, such as the floribunda 'City of Leeds', had already gone over. Although there were many 'blind' (flowerless) shoots because of some sharp frosts at the end of April and the beginning of May, there were far fewer split centres than usual. Although there would still be enough floribundas in flower for the Northern Show, it looked as if the hybrid teas might be a little sparse. The men comforted themselves with the thought that southern growers would be in a worse state and they anticipated that some faces would be absent from the Lakeland Rose Show, held in 1989 on 15 and 16 July.

Don, Jennie and Tom cut the roses the day before the show. Don is usually up at five o'clock in the morning and begins as soon as possible, and Tom joins him at York Crescent by half past six. They cut the roses, leaving stems as long as possible, and put them immediately into buckets of water. They continually bear in mind which classes they are entering, and it is the consistent concentration on what is required which makes this day such hard, and often tense, work. They are also conscious that they will need roses of different stem lengths for the large bowls and vases. The height of the car is a limiting factor but they are experienced enough to gauge that too. When the buckets are full, the roses are decanted into the special home-made travel crates, either at the gardens or in the garage at home.

The travelling crates are of their own devising and most ingenious. They contain plastic tubes which hold water. Into each of these is placed a rose which is fastened individually to one of the thin wooden battens which run across the top of the crate. Infinite care is taken with this task because the petals can so easily be bruised or torn.

Time presses because the roses lose water progressively through the day so must be cut in the morning if possible, particularly in hot weather. Tom takes his roses back to his garage in Seaton Carew to sort out; he has fewer roses to choose than Don and he does not prepare the two specimen bloom boxes at home (he and Don disagree about this, as in little else) so he usually has time for some rest before he and Iris set out at about midnight for the Lake District.

The last roses arrive at the Charltons' garage at about three o'clock in the afternoon. This is the moment of truth, when the 'specimen blooms' for the 'boxes' are chosen, cut down, measured with a ruler, and then placed into the home-made boxes with lids in which they will travel to the show. Specimen blooms are particularly big hybrid tea roses at the peak of development and three-quarters open. There are several classes specifically for them. They differ only in size and age, however, from those hybrid tea roses put in the 'large-flowered' classes, which are usually younger and therefore fresher. 'Cutting

them [the stems] down is always the hard part, because once they're cut, they can't go into a vase or a bowl.' Before they go they make up three 'boxes': for eighteen, twelve and six distinct varieties.

Without stalks, and set in 'boxes', the connection between these huge specimens and ordinary garden roses seems tenuous; yet the 'box' classes are the most prestigious of all rose classes. First prize for the 'box of eighteen' is £18. When they arrive at the show tent, they will be put in the RNRS 'staging boards'. These have superseded exhibition 'boxes' but they are still known by the old name.

When sorting out roses, particularly those destined for the 'box' classes, Don and Tom may indulge in a little 'dressing'. Most rose exhibitors practise 'dressing' to a greater or lesser extent. This is the technique whereby a young hybrid tea flower is aged or an old flower kept back; the first is achieved by the skilful use of fingers or cotton wool, the second by soft knitting wool. 'Dressing' is the word also used to refer to the removal of the very outer petals, called the 'guard' petals, if they are damaged in any way. It is a very skilful process demanding a great deal of experience for if it is overdone the judges (who know quite well what goes on) may mark an exhibit down. They certainly will if any cotton wool is left after staging, so the canny exhibitor puts in cotton wool which is a different colour from the flower and so is easily distinguished in the dim light of a marquee at night. Don, according to Tom, is immensely skilled at 'dressing'. 'He makes it look so easy but it's an art.' Tom is no slouch at 'dressing' either, but neither bothers to hold back an older rose using knitting wool as was often done in the past. As far as they are concerned, a rose held back will not have that freshness and colour that they are looking for. 'Dressing' is not considered to be cheating, simply gilding the lily. Rose exhibitors certainly do not go to the lengths of chrysanthemum showmen, who will spend more than an hour tweaking every one of the many petals of a large mop-headed chrysanthemum with a pair of tweezers, often undermining its individual character in the process.

After all is prepared by about 8 o'clock the Charltons then pack up and leave for the showground. They usually arrive at about two thirty in the morning and start staging at three o'clock. They have until a quarter to nine to stage, when the tent will be cleared for the judging to begin at nine o'clock. They know they will have to stage, apart from the three 'box' classes, one multi-vase exhibit (three vases of six roses, each vase of a different variety); a separate vase of six specimen blooms; a bowl of twelve large-flowered all the same; a bowl of eighteen, six distinct varieties; a bowl of twelve, six varieties; a 'Star' specimen bloom class, and a 'three stage' bloom. In the floribunda section there is a class for one bowl of twelve

Don's successful 'box' of eighteen, *all* distinct varieties.
To win this class is the apogee of the serious exhibitor's ambition.

stems; three vases of not more than five stems, separate varieties; and a bowl of twelve stems, four varieties. In the miniature rose classes, open to all exhibitors, there is a bowl (any number of stems); three vases of five; a basket; a 'box', and an 'artist's palette'. It is a list to make the head swim. 'When you think about that lot you understand why there is pressure on us.' In reality, although they put each class on the entry form, there is not usually enough time, or energy, to stage everything. The floribunda classes are the casualties of limited time.

Tom will be staging a 'Star' class for a specimen bloom; a 'box' of twelve specimen blooms; a 'box' of six specimen blooms, four or more varieties; and a vase of six specimen blooms. In the large-flowered classes, he will stage a bowl of twelve, six varieties; a vase of six stems, two varieties; three vases of six; and a 'three stage' bloom.

In the floribunda section he will enter the classes for a bowl of twelve stems, four varieties, and three vases of three. He will enter four miniature rose classes for those with 75 varieties or less: a bowl, any number of stems; three vases of three stems; a vase of six stems, two varieties; and a basket with any number of stems. If he has any roses over he may enter one or two of the classes in the Lakeland Champion competition.

The receptacles are provided by the RNRS, thus eliminating the possibility of exhibitors being disqualified because their bowls are of the wrong dimensions, a common occurrence at local shows. There is, however, a heartfelt sentence in Don Charlton's book on the subject: *'The rose bowls provided by many shows come complete with a grid which is supposed to hold stems in place, but it tends to turn the staging operation into more of an engineering feat than an art. Discard these grids and use a staging medium [i.e. 'oasis' or cut reeds] instead.'*

However taxing growing roses for shows can be, nothing is quite as demanding as staging them at a national show. Just after arrival at the showground is the worst time, according to Jennie. 'That's when you're really sick of them [the roses]. You've been working with them then almost twenty-four hours and you feel terrible and you want to go to bed and that's when I feel Oh, I'm fed up.' She says that she finds people want to come up and talk to her but she finds that a waste of time, because the more exhibits they can get put up, the more relaxed she becomes knowing she knows there is less work to do at the end.

'I once got into serious trouble at Lakeland', admits Don. They had transported twelve stems of 'Iceberg' (a floribunda) because Don had insisted Jennie put them in at Billingham. At about four thirty in the morning Don's tolerance was low and he decided he was not going to stage the 'Iceberg'. Jennie decided that he was. And he did. And they won. 'And I was never allowed to live that one down.' 'He said, when we were packing, that we'd need the 'Iceberg' – we had something like thirty-seven floribunda stems. Then he lost interest in all the floribundas because Don's first love is the hybrid teas. So he said he wouldn't stage them all.' Jennie replied that she had not brought them all that way for him not to 'something well' stage them. She went out to the car to do something and when she got back, there the 'Iceberg' were, beautifully staged. And a very calm voice said, 'Just make out a ticket for 'Iceberg', will you?'

In these matters the exhibitor at national level who is staging all night is at a considerable disadvantage compared to those who go to local shows, for tiredness undoubtedly causes mistakes. Numbers of roses are miscounted, the wrong size of vase for the class is selected, and extraneous elements like cotton wool pellets are left in the roses to irritate or amuse the judges, depending on their temperament. Don is well known for his capacity for misreading the schedule when exhausted and quite often suffers the indignity of 'NAS' written across his entry card.

In a way large shows are only village shows writ large. They are subject to the same mishaps and miscalculations. One night at Holker Hall (where the rose show was held until 1987), one of the park deer got close to the tent and ate the heads off some magnificent roses in a bucket left temporarily outside. Once it rained so hard that the water cascaded into the tent and exploded a light bulb and the exhibitors had to pick pieces of glass out of the roses. There have been times when the rain has come through the tent and it has been possible to fill the vases more quickly standing under the drips than from the taps. And, like a village show, the Lakeland Show is well liked by the exhibitors for the friendliness of the organizers; they are particularly grateful for the cups of coffee brought to them in the middle of the night.

The attraction of the rose for Don and Tom (and other exhibitors) undoubtedly lies not only in the challenge of growing them well but in their 'classic' shape. Ordinary amateur gardeners, on the other hand, are increasingly turning to roses of the 'old-fashioned' type.

Exhibitors, including Don and Tom, are also less concerned about the scent of roses than their shape, although fragrance undoubtedly appeals to the public who come to flower shows. Indeed many show roses have no scent at all, it having been largely ignored in the past in the quest for larger flowers and other characteristics ('Admiral Rodney' being a shining exception to this general proposition). Scent is hardly a consideration for Don, in any event, because only about three times a year does he have any sense of smell.

There are straws in the wind, however. Although there will always be classes where size and 'classic' form are most important, the RNRS sensed a shift of emphasis amongst its membership some years ago and has introduced more classes for ordinary garden roses, new and old (from which the very large-flowered roses like 'Admiral Rodney', 'Big Chief', 'Jan Guest' and 'Red Devil' are expressly excluded). There is also a class specifically for scented roses. These classes are not likely to interest the serious exhibitors very much, of course, because for them garden decoration and appeal is decidedly secondary. It is the search for absolute perfection in colour, form, and condition which matters. In any event, at present at least, points gained in the classes for garden roses cannot contribute towards winning the championship.

Although change of this kind may seem irrelevant to the serious exhibitors, changes in judging criteria are not.

Don's winning bowl of twelve 'Red Devil' hybrid tea roses,
arranged in the most decorative way.

The judges are no longer looking for the same things as twenty years ago. As Don puts it: 'The main difference is the quality and cleanliness of the blooms has improved two or three hundred per cent . . . Their [the judges'] attitude to the exhibition "box" and specimen bloom . . . has changed. That's all to the good . . . If they [the roses] are old or wan there is a place for them and it's either the compost heap or the waste bin.' *A propos* staging: 'I'm afraid in the old days, roses were almost haphazardly put into the vases and bowls. Now they are much fresher and arranged in a more pleasing way – better spacing, balance, and shape to the exhibit overall.' Although he would no doubt deny it, Don must take much of the credit for the staging of younger, fresher flowers.

The staging of floribundas and miniatures has changed too. Because they are not protected by bloom covers, the presentation is all important to distinguish between them. 'The old system [of showing floribundas] was to bunch together the colour so that there was no spacing between the trusses and you had a solid mass of bloom. Thrown together mainly and usually they appeared to be walking on stilts. . . . With the new régime. . . the flower is not almost down to the bowl neck and we have an oval or round arrangement . . . which has got some form and curvature.'

With regard to miniature roses, Don believes that there was a lot of confusion – and still is – after the initial rules were laid down by the RNRS. They were not interpreted by the judges or exhibitors in the way intended. Primarily, miniature roses are tiny and dainty; they should be arranged so that they are well spaced. He feels 'boxes' should only be used for miniatures with a classic HT form. 'We now have classes for the "Artist's Palette" which caters for the miniature rose with fewer petals that opens up bright and fresh and shows its stamens. . . The bowls and vases will incorporate roses of

either type but my personal preference would be for roses which are half to three-quarters open, fresh and bright and daintily arranged . . . Given that, the miniature rose will become even more popular than it is today. The numbers of exhibits has increased almost ten-fold over the last five years.'

The week before the Lakeland Show in 1989, at St Albans, Don and Tom won the Southern Championship in their respective sections and an 'Admiral Rodney' of Don's won 'Best Bloom in Show'. So, although the flush was nearly at an end, the signs were good for success at the Lakeland Rose Show to be held for the first time on a site near Cark-in-Cartmel in Cumbria.

Because there were fewer roses to choose from, the Charltons and Fosters arrived at the showground much earlier than usual so that staging was a longer and more leisurely affair.

In the end it proved to be a successful, if hot, day for both Tom and Don. By the end of the judging, Don had extended his lead over his rivals so that it would take a considerable effort for anyone to beat him in the Great Autumn Rose Show, to be held for the first time in Birmingham. He was fifty-two points ahead and only

Tom's successful three vases of six hybrid tea roses, each a distinct variety: from the front they are 'Admiral Rodney', 'Red Devil', and 'Grandpa Dickson'.

sixty five points were on offer in the autumn. Tom's position was already unassailable. Tom's pleasure in his victory was slightly marred by two incidents, however. One was a slip he made when preparing his entry for the Lakeland Challenge Trophy which requires nine floribunda stems in four varieties in a bowl. He inadvertently put in only eight, an easy mistake to make with floribundas which have so many flower heads.

The other was more irritating. At St Albans, he had put in a basket of miniature roses, covered in flower 'like a football', thinking that was what was required. He was awarded first prize. At Lakeland he displayed them similarly in a class with two entries and he was only awarded second prize; the other entry came third. It was plain the judges were looking for a more airy arrangement of blooms. The difference in judging criteria applied upset him very much. The problem is that miniature roses are newcomers to rose shows and the judges are not yet fully *ad idem* over the best way of marking them. Since then agreement has been reached as to how to judge miniature roses in baskets, but it came too late to save Tom from annoyance.

In the autumn show, held in early September, although there were no floribundas to show because the second flush was not really yet under way and they had to show some young blooms, the two men from Billingham, the north-east's 'likely lads' as they are known to the readers of *Garden News*, won their respective championships. They took home no cups, however, because, as Jennie says, 'the novelty of polishing cups wore off years ago, and anyway, there's no room in the car.

Few flower enthusiasts are prepared to go to such lengths in pursuit of excellence – to the point where differences between the exhibits is so finely judged as to pass unnoticed amongst the general public and where the rule book reigns supreme. The sacrifices required are considerable and I sensed that there would come a time in the not-too-distant future when the Chalrtons and the Fosters would no longer be prepared to endure the discomfort, lack of sleep and long-distance travel imposed on national exhibitors by the exigencies of show organization; let alone the enormous amount of work required to cultivate roses to such a high standard.

Both Don and Tom feel that they should continue to compete, even though they are the acknowledged champions, in order to maintain a standard and to give fellow-competitors incentive. 'When you reach the pinnacle, eveybody wants to knock you off.' However, Don is beginning to wonder whether, if he were to win the championship ten times, he might not then review the situation. 'People don't realize how much effort is necessary to keep up that standard for a prolonged period. It takes a lot of the summer of every year.' I should say that was admirably understated.

As gardeners in shrunken gardens turn more to specialisms, such as alpines or fuchsias, those shows which cater for these are thriving and should continue to do so. So, too, are the local agricultural shows where the rewards, both financial and prestigious, in the rearing of good livestock, together with an increasing interest in country life as it disappears before our eyes, ensure their continuing popularity. However, the future of the small unspecialist flower show is more uncertain.

It seems to me that rapid social and economic developments both make this show more important – to help reconcile the old-established order to change, and to draw in the newcomers – and may threaten its survival in the long term. Yet survive it must. Not only to help ensure that crafts perfected over generations do not die out – as Philip Larkin put it in 'Show Saturday', for the *'pure excellences that enclose a recession of skills'*, but because the flower show is a classless and unifying social occasion: *'something they* [the people] *share that breaks ancestrally each year into regenerate union'*. It is for those reasons that I would echo Larkin's concluding plea: *'Let it always be there.'*

List of Useful Organisations

British Fuchsia Society
29 Princes Crescent, Dollar, Clackmannanshire.

British Cactus and Succulent Society
4 Hargate Close, Summerseat, Bury, Lancs. BL9 5NU.

Fruit Group of the Royal Horticultural Society
RHS, Vincent Square, London SW1P 2PE.

National Association of Flower Arrangement Societies of Great Britain
21 Denbigh Street, London SW1V 2HF.

National Begonia Society
4 Shackelton View, Cubley, Penistone, S. Yorks S30 6HT

National Sweet Pea Society
3 Chalk Farm Road, Stokenchurch, High Wycombe, Bucks HP14 3TB.

National Vegetable Society
56 Waun-y-Groes Avenue, Rhiwbina, Cardiff, S. Glamorgan.

Royal Caledonian Horticultural Society
2 Buckstone Way, Edinburgh.

Royal Horticultural Society
80 Vincent Square, London SW1 2PE.

Royal Horticultural Society of Ireland
Swanbrook House, Bloomfield Avenue, Donnybrook, Dublin 4.

The Royal National Rose Society
Chiswell Green, St. Albans, Herts. AL2 3NR.

National Society of Allotment and Leisure Gardeners
Hunters Road, Corby, Northants NN1T 1JE.

INDEX